Praise for *America's Forgotten Majority*

"Teixeira and Rogers have written an exceptionally important book on how American politics has deserted half the electorate. The revival—or continuing decay—of progressive politics literally depends on whether political leaders take the insights of this book to heart."

—Robert Kuttner, Co-Editor, *The American Prospect*

"Two of the best minds for deep political analysis—Ruy Teixeira and Joel Rogers—have blown away the fog of fashionable punditry and led us back to clearer ground. The vital, missing core of any progressive agenda remains the neglected white working class and this book explains why and how the Democratic Party must regain their allegiance if it expects to govern successfully."

—William Greider, National Affairs Correspondent, *The Nation*

"Teixeira and Rogers make a strong political and economic case for paying more attention to the needs of the white working class, and creating a coalition between them and the poor. Here's a book every concerned citizen should read, and every aspiring politician should take to heart.

—Robert B. Reich, University Professor and Hexter Professor of Social and Economic Policy, Heller School, Brandeis University

"Few people understand the numbers of American politics better than Ruy Teixeira and few bring them to life more intelligently and vividly. Teixeira and Joel Rogers remind us that understanding American politics requires us to understand the hopes and aspirations of working Americans who don't get much attention in trendy circles, but make the country run."

—E. J. Dionne, author of *Why Americans Hate Politics*

"Ruy Teixeira and Joel Rogers have well-deserved reputations for looking closely at demographic and political data and interpreting it in provocative, convincing ways. This new book clarifies many previously undiscussed aspects of the politics and culture of America's second Gilded Age. It will be valuable during the 2000 election campaign and beyond."

—James Fallows, author of *Breaking the News*

"Teixeira and Rogers have it right. In this rare and insightful book, these two experts point the way to a new majority, reaching across historic battlegrounds to find economic common ground. They provide a map for the people's movement to follow."

—Rev. Jesse L. Jackson, Sr.

"Whenever I have to write an article about political opinion, the first person I call is Ruy Teixeira. He's my secret weapon. But now the secret will be out. In a new book written with Joel Rogers, Teixeira challenges the conventional wisdom about politics by arguing that the next great realignment in American politics will pivot on the allegiance of downscale white workers rather than upscale soccer moms. Anyone thinking about the future of American politics will want to read this book."

—John B. Judis, Senior Editor of *The New Republic* and author of *The Paradox of American Democracy*

"Timely and trenchant . . . . The authors argue that the media and political community in general have talked too much about boutique elements of the electorate while ignoring its core."

—Ronald Elving, *The Washington Post*

"Ruy Teixeira and Joel Rogers demonstrate in the important new book *America's Forgotten Majority* [that] working class whites have . . . been the key to Democratic prospects over the past decade . . . may provide the theoretical rationale for the Gore campaign in much the same way E. J. Dionne's *Why Americans Hate Politics* did for Clinton's 1992 candidacy."

—Harold Meyerson, *L.A. Weekly*

"*America's Forgotten Majority* . . . an agenda for the New New Democrat."

—Tod Lindberg, *Washington Times*

"Teixeira and Rogers have put together a powerful array of data and statistics demonstrating the pivotal role of this critical group, and their argument in behalf of the white working class should be closely studied by all those who seek to influence national politics . . . Teixeira and Rogers have made a significant contribution to the political debate in identifying both the broad scope of Democratic losses among once loyal voters, and the suffering such voters have experienced as their livelihoods have been threatened and as their families stressed by downward pressures on the working-class male wage. To restore the vitality of a left coalition will clearly require effective political appeals targeted to America's white non-college-educated majority."

—Thomas Edsall, *Dissent*

"There's a chance that Teixeira and Rogers have helped do for the Democrats what Kevin Phillips's "Southern strategy" did for the Republicans in 1968 and beyond."

—Jack Metzgar, *The Nation*

"This book deserves to have had the influence it has. In less than 200 pages, it focuses attention on the voters who have been the key to the Republican presidential majority of the last 32 years and the Republican congressional majorities of the last six. It's one of those rare works that's a must-read if you want to be part of the argument about electoral politics today."

—James Chapin, United Press International
National Political Analyst

"Teixeira and Rogers's *America's Forgotten Majority* is stuffed with factoid treasures that will correct many political misperceptions."

—Christopher Caldwell, *Weekly Standard*

"Teixeira . . . and Rogers . . . argue persuasively that [the white working class] was actually the swing bloc in recent national elections—just as it was in the days when blue-collar workers who voted Republican were called Nixon Democrats and, later, Reagan Democrats . . . . Neither party, warns *America's Forgotten Majority*, has a platform that speaks directly to white workers. If they do hold the swing vote, the future is up for grabs."

—Aaron Bernstein, *Business Week*

"The future of American politics belongs to the party best able to win the hearts and minds of the white working class: that is Teixeira and Rogers's thesis in a well-documented analysis of the current American political landscape that is coherent, insightful and refreshingly contrary to the prevailing views of Sunday morning pundits and politicos of both major parties . . . the authors . . . build a convincing case that white working-class voters, not the recently fabled soccer moms, were, and will be again, the true swing voters."
—*Publishers Weekly*

"As University of Wisconsin Professor Joel Rogers and Ruy Teixeira show in their brilliant new book, *America's Forgotten Majority*, the true swing voters—particularly in the Midwestern states, where the election will be decided—are nonunion, noncollege-educated, middle- and low-income whites—waitress moms, not soccer moms."
—Robert Borosage, *Washington Post*

AMERICA'S FORGOTTEN MAJORITY

AMERICA'S FORGOTTEN MAJORITY

Why the White Working Class Still Matters

RUY TEIXEIRA

JOEL ROGERS

A New Republic Book

BASIC
BOOKS

A Member of the Perseus Books Group

Published by Basic Books,
A Member of the Perseus Books Group

FIRST PAPERBACK EDITION

Designed by Rachel Hegarty

Teixeira, Ruy A.
    America's forgotten majority : why the white working class still matters/ Ruy Teixeira & Joel Rogers.
        p. cm.
    Includes bibliographical references and index.
    ISBN 0–465–08399–4
    1. Working class whites—United States—Political activity. 2. Elections—United States. 3. United States—Politics and government—1993– I. Rogers, Joel, 1952– II. Title.

HD8076 .T49 2000
305.5'62'089034073—dc21

                                                                        00-027791

01 02 03 04 10 9 8 7 6 5 4 3 2 1

What the people want is very simple. They want an America as good as its promise.

—BARBARA JORDAN

CONTENTS

PREFACE

T HE READER WHO HAS PICKED UP THIS BOOK may wonder at first why we have chosen to write a book focusing on the plight of the white working class. At face value, a book with such a focus could be seen as either very narrowly cast, given long-term demographic trends, or (more distressingly) as reactionary or racist in intent. In fact, the origins of this book lie in our concern that most Americans' hopes and expectations for their government have become unnecessarily limited. If one were to believe the bulk of news stories, the typical American voters these days are affluent white mothers (in 1996 they were called "soccer moms") and fathers, living in the suburbs and probably involved in the information economy (as "wired workers"), whose interest in government reflects their relatively privileged position: "No big programs, please, because we don't really need them, but small, inexpensive ones are OK, provided they target one of our few remaining problems." If this characterization is truly accurate, perhaps the extraordinarily cautious and modest nature of today's politics has a solid justification. Large social and economic problems cannot be tackled because the average voter is too far removed from them.

But if this characterization is not accurate, perhaps we are unnecessarily downgrading the role of government and selling the future of our country short. This possibility occurred to us as we pored over accounts of elections in the 1990s and became increasingly suspicious that conventional stereotypes of the American voter couldn't possibly be accurate. We knew, for example, that over three-quarters of American adults do not have a four-year college degree, that over seven-tenths do not have a professional or managerial job, and that the median—typical—income of American households was actually quite modest (in 1998, about $39,000). Could American voters, in general, and swing voters, in particular, really be that different? Could it really be true that, as one newspaper story put it, "Nixon's Silent Majority and the Reagan Democrats . . . are becoming as hard to find . . . as parking spots at the local minimall"?[1]

We became particularly intrigued by the assertion—sometimes explicit (as in the example above), sometimes implicit, but almost always there—that the white working class had become politically irrelevant. How could this be? The 1980s weren't that long ago. Demographic change is generally gradual, not sudden. The country is still mostly white (a term that describes almost three-quarters of adults and more than four-fifths of voters), and the majority of people (according to the data just cited) have a job, an education, and an income that could broadly be described as working class.

Well, what can't be usually isn't. As the above-mentioned data might lead one to expect, the white working class is alive and well in American politics today. Sure, a large proportion prefers the label "middle class" and doesn't toil in factories or do any other kind of blue-collar work. But its economic position in American society bears little resemblance to that of the suburban college-educated professionals about whom we hear so much.

We call these white working-class voters the "forgotten majority" of American politics: "forgotten" both because we haven't heard much about them of late and because they haven't benefited much from policy changes of the last thirty years or so; "majority" because they are just that—about 55 percent of the voting population. In this book we make two basic arguments about these voters.

First, however you play with the numbers, making varying assumptions about voter mobilization and partisan allegiance, it's next to impossible to cement a dominant electoral coalition without capturing the support of a good share of the forgotten majority. So a party that wants to win has to remember them and offer them something concrete. And a party that wants to get reelected by them and dominate over the long term has to offer them some very substantial changes.

Second, the changes that these voters really want—and that aren't being offered in sufficient quantities by either of the major parties at present—are improvements in basic aspects of their lives. They have a multitude of difficulties and concerns that the "new economy"—as well as it has performed in the last several years—is highly unlikely to solve on its own. The health insurance situation is becoming more, not less, precarious. Providing for a secure retirement is becoming more, not less, difficult. Getting the right education and training is becoming more challenging, even as it becomes more important. Resolving the tensions between work and family life is becoming more daunting with every passing year. Competing in a global economy is making it harder, not easier, to ensure one's family a decent standard of living. These are high-stakes issues for voters who don't have a wide margin for error in their lives—and, again, not even a booming economy (itself a transitory phenomenon) is going to solve them.

Which basically leaves government.

Here the picture that emerges from the forgotten majority is a little more complicated. It is true that the members of this majority are currently suspicious of government—though less so today than in the recent past—but they're not particularly ideological about that. In other words, they don't dislike government on principle. They even recognize that government action is needed to address many of their problems. But what they know is that government has done very little for them in the last several decades, and they question whether that is truly changing now—whether government could again be made to work for them.

Turning that last attitude around will certainly be a challenge. But it's a challenge that's clearly more tractable than trying to sell strong government to those who are opposed to it on principle or have little need for it. It's as if white working-class voters would like to be convinced that government could really do big things for them. They're just waiting for someone to make that argument, and that offer, in a compelling way. And the numbers tell us that any party that does so will dominate American politics in the future, with a popular base for a new and bolder approach to government.

What About Minority Voters?

As alluded to above, the reader may initially find it strange that we focus so much on white voters, particularly in a book arguing about a possible return to strong government. What about the concerns and interests of minorities, particularly blacks and Hispanics? Haven't they been "forgotten" by recent public policy in many of the same ways as working-class whites? Wouldn't their support be integral to any return to strong government? For that matter, wouldn't minority voters probably be the strongest supporters of such a shift and the ones who would benefit the most if it happened?

Absolutely. And that's why the focus on white voters—forgotten majority voters—is so important, even for those primarily concerned about problems in the minority community. Minority voters cannot drive a return to strong government alone. There are simply not enough of them. But if forgotten majority voters are really the swing voters in American politics and share a broad set of problems with minority voters, it's suddenly a new ballgame. Rather than being isolated in one corner of American politics, while affluent soccer moms and wired workers supposedly dictate a cautious and conservative agenda, minority voters, with enough forgotten majority support, can potentially put a strong universalist program—around issues like health, retirement, education, and economic security—squarely in the center of political debate.

Of course, we are well aware of the long history of racism in the United States, and of the fact that shared "material interests" have often proved insufficient to bring voters of different colors together. Nor do we have any illusions that today's white working class is completely free of racial antagonisms. But we also believe that enormous progress has been made in racial attitudes over the past two generations and that shared material interests remain an excellent basis on which to start political alliances. In fact, without these shared interests, it's difficult to get started at all.

The reader might also think it strange that we are focusing on a group of white voters when the country itself is becoming so diverse. Won't natural processes of demographic change eventually make it untenable to highlight the role of such voters? Not for a long time. As mentioned above, today almost three-quarters of the adults and over four-fifths of the voters in this country are white. These ratios will change only slowly in the 21st century. Population projections suggest that by the middle of the century, five decades from now, 56 percent of adults (and probably over three-fifths of voters) will still be white. So, we are becoming more diverse, but not so fast that politics in the early 21st century will not depend heavily on the views and inclinations of white voters—particularly the forgotten majority voters whom we focus on in this book.

Finally, the reader might wonder whether the pervasive influence of money in politics makes our argument correct on the level of electoral arithmetic but irrelevant in the real world of

American policy making. The forgotten majority might indeed be the key ingredient in future electoral coalitions, but the policy agenda of the nation will be driven not by their interests, or those of other rank-and-file voters, but rather by the interests of people who have the money to buy access to politicians. We acknowledge that money in politics is a problem but believe that the popular base for strong government remains tremendously important and potentially decisive. Indeed, without such a popular base, it's really not possible to go against the interests of determined and well-connected economic interests who might well oppose that approach to government. And the need for that popular base brings us straight back to a politics that clearly embraces the interests of forgotten majority voters.

We want to stress that the content of that politics is our chief concern. We are not simply making an argument about how to construct an electoral majority, though that is certainly part of our analysis. We are making an argument about America's future. This country need not content itself with a minimalist government that does little to solve its most serious problems. There is nothing in the structure of today's electorate that should lead one to that conclusion. If politicians have the courage to address the needs of America's forgotten majority with a strong, universalist program, we can cast off the shackles hobbling government today and finally achieve a truly inclusive national greatness.

America's Forgotten Majority

ONE

Introducing America's Forgotten Majority— And Why It Is the Key to Our Political Future

Dewey Burton has become a happy man, and he will gladly vote for Ronald Reagan for President on November 4. He is 34 years old, short and bull-shouldered, with a gap-toothed grin. An energetic worker at a Ford Motor Company assembly plant in suburban Detroit that turns out luxury Lincoln Continentals and Mark VI's, he is a strong union man, a Democrat by upbringing and conviction.

— *New York Times,* OCTOBER 15, 1980

IN THE 1970S AND 1980S, white working-class voters were recognized as the key swing voters of American electoral politics, and they swung against the Democratic party. Figures like the iconic "Joe Sixpack" or TV's Archie Bunker—white, blue-collar, culturally conservative men who were fed up with the Democrats and their various "liberal" causes, which in their view included something for everyone but them—would by the Reagan years come to symbolize those who sent the Democrats down in flames.

But now, as we enter a new century, politics is different, isn't it? Time has passed Joe Sixpack by. Manufacturing employment has declined. A "new economy" has arisen. America has become more diverse and socially tolerant, even as it has become more conservative economically and less expectant of help from government. Old Democrats are out. New Democrats are in. Joe Sixpack and his working-class concerns no longer affect election outcomes.

The new swing voters, it is said, are affluent suburbanites who are riding the wave of the new economy—"soccer moms," the stars of the 1996 elections, and "wired workers" whose concerns are light-years removed from blue-collar life. Since swing voters are the voters politicians must concentrate on—most voters lean clearly toward either the Republicans or Democrats in any given election and thus are much less in play—it is these affluent suburbanites whose interests are decisively shaping today's politics. Newspaper reports from the 1996 election onward tell the story.

> Soccer moms . . . were America's most wanted voters and their every wish turned up on some politician's list of promises: child tax credits, education tax breaks, scholarships, V-chips, school uniforms, longer childbirth stays, time off for teacher conferences, even a breast cancer web site. Some called it pandering, others family friendliness. (*USA Today*, November 6, 1996)

> Wired workers are the wave of the future, political analysts say. Political parties will learn to surf the new demographics, or go under. Wired workers solve problems as part of self-directed teams and regularly use computers on the job. They tend to be self-reliant, mobile, affluent, pro–free market, socially tolerant and deeply concerned about educating their children and re-educating themselves. And they are multiplying. (*Tulsa World*, October 28, 1998)

Suburbs vary immensely, of course ... [b]ut politicians use the term as collective shorthand for key groups of swing voters: married couples with children, the "soccer moms" who were so sought after in the 1996 election, affluent independent voters and the high-technology employees who work miles from any city." (*New York Times*, May 4, 1999)

The interests of these new swing voters are helping drive a political environment marked by

- a general lack of political support for significant public spending, including investment in public goods like education, infrastructure, and health care;
- a lack of concern about economic inequality, despite a widening gap between rich and poor;
- pressures to privatize Social Security—the signature program of the New Deal and chief source of retirement security for most workers;
- an overriding commitment to fiscal austerity (even with the budget not only in balance but in *surplus*, there is little pressure to engage in significant new spending);
- the rise of less patient-friendly managed care, and continued increases in the ranks of the uninsured, but little political pressure for comprehensive health-care reform;
- a general reverence for the market and a concomitant disdain for the federal government, especially large-scale federal programs;
- a relatively free rein for large corporations, coupled with low esteem for organized labor; and
- a commitment to free trade above other economic goals such as raising living standards.

And, we are told, given the dominance of these new swing voters, the future of American politics promises more of the same.

The 21st century will be an era of limited government, tight budgets, and reliance on private markets to solve social problems. The only real question is how much of this we'll get and in what combination we'll get it. That's the way these swing voters see it, so we're stuck with it, right?

Wrong. In this book, we show that the real "swing" voters remain the same white working-class men and women who've always been the ballast of America's active electorate—but who, given recent policy and media neglect, have effectively become a "forgotten majority." Members of this majority—about 55 percent of the voting population—don't much resemble Joe Sixpack in their cultural attitudes today. But neither do they resemble the affluent soccer moms and dads or "wired" professionals beloved by media commentators. And over the past generation, they have actually lost, not gained, economic ground.

In what follows we argue two things. First, the forgotten majority's economic difficulties over the last several decades, and the political parties' failure to address them successfully, have a central role in explaining recent trends in American voting—including the long-term decline in support for activist government and the volatility of support for either major party. Second, the forgotten majority, whose concerns can't be assuaged by the political agenda sketched above, has the numbers to anchor a dominant new political coalition, but will do so only if their concerns are addressed directly and effectively. Should either of the major parties, or even a new one, such as the Reform party, seize that opportunity, our future may in fact look quite different from what the conventional wisdom today insists it must.

America's Forgotten Majority in Historical Context

[Republican strategist Glen] Bolger said that that next year, the Republican and Democratic Presidential nominees will try to

> target swing female voters ... the so-called soccer moms—
> white, suburban, married women.
>
> — *Omaha World-Herald*, AUGUST 7, 1999

One important thing to keep in mind is how historically odd the current enshrinement of soccer moms and wired workers is. From the New Deal through the 1980s, it was widely recognized that white working-class voters were, in one way or another, the key to American politics. To be sure, there were important divisions among white working-class voters—by country of origin (German, Scandinavian, Eastern European, English, Irish, etc.), by religion (Protestants versus Catholics), and by region (South versus non-South)—that greatly complicated the politics of this group, but the quest for electoral success depended on mastering these complications and maintaining a deep base among these voters.

The New Deal Coalition, for example, as originally forged, included most blacks and was certainly cross-class, especially among groups such as Jews and southerners. The prototypical member of the coalition, however, was an ethnic white worker— commonly visualized as working in a unionized factory, but also including those who weren't in unions or who toiled in other blue-collar settings (construction, transportation, etc.). It was these voters who provided the numbers for four FDR election victories and Harry Truman's narrow victory in 1948[1] and who provided political support for the emerging U.S. welfare state, with its implicit social contract and greatly expanded role for government.

Even in the 1950s, with Republican Dwight Eisenhower as president, the white working class provided the margin of victory in two elections. And it was the white working class who continued to support the expansion of the welfare state, as a roaring U.S. economy continued to deliver the goods and government continued to pour money into roads, science, schools, and whatever else seemed necessary to build up the country. This era, stretching back into the late 1940s and forward to the mid-1960s, was the one that created the first mass middle class in the world—a middle class that even factory workers could enter, since they could earn a relatively comfortable living even without high levels of education or professional skills. A middle class, in other words, that members of the white working class could reasonably aspire to and frequently attain.

Things began to fall apart in the 1960s. Though the white working class supported both Kennedy and Johnson and the liberalism of that era, up to a point, its support became qualified by the emergence of conflicts around race (initially, riots and the rise of militant black nationalism; later, affirmative action and busing to achieve racial balance) and the Vietnam War.[2] These conflicts led directly to the triumph of Richard Nixon in 1968 and a stunningly high vote (14 percent) for third-party candidate George Wallace, as disaffected white working-class voters deserted the Democratic party en masse (64 percent voted for either Nixon or Wallace).

White working-class voters were also widely acknowledged to be the force behind the massive popular rejection of George McGovern in 1972, as an overwhelming 70 percent of this group cast their ballots for Nixon. The Democrats of course came back under Carter, but it was a short respite as dissatisfaction mounted with slow economic growth and high inflation in the late 1970s— conditions that suddenly cast doubt on ordinary workers' ability to attain or sustain a middle-class standard of living.

Dissatisfaction with the Democrats crystallized in the election of 1980, as Ronald Reagan soundly defeated Carter's bid for a second term. And the driving force once again was white working-class voters who found Reagan's anti-tax, small-government message appealing in an era when the government seemed to be doing less and less for them (57 percent voted for Reagan, just 34 percent for Carter). This time they even had a name: *Reagan Democrats*. Typically conceptualized as white ethnics who lived in blue-collar, Democratic areas like Macomb County, Michigan—site of a famous study of Reagan Democrats by Democratic pollster Stanley Greenberg—they were said to have shed their historical loyalty to the Democrats, perhaps permanently, to vote for Reagan and embrace his anti-government message. Of course, the Reagan Democrat phenomenon was broader than this, but the image served to clarify in the public mind and political debate the kind of swing voters Reagan had managed to reach.

And those white working-class swing voters stuck with the Republicans through two more presidential elections: Reagan achieved a landslide reelection victory in 1984, followed by George Bush's decisive defeat of Michael Dukakis in 1988. The stage was set, in the view of many observers, for an era of uninterrupted Republican domination, based on the consolidation of the Reagan Democrats in the GOP column.

That was not to be. Now the 1990s have ended and the Democrats have won the last two presidential elections, though the Republicans still control Congress after their stunning victory in 1994. And, all of a sudden, the white working class is nowhere to be found in most media accounts of current politics. After dominating our politics for sixty years, they are conspicuous by their absence. We hear a lot about soccer moms, wired workers, suburban independents, and so on—but virtually nothing about this formerly central group of voters.

What happened? Has the world really changed so much in the last decade or two? Could the white working class have been rendered irrelevant by the rise of a new economy to the point where it just doesn't matter anymore?

The Working Class in the New Economy

It's certainly true that there have been fundamental shifts in the American economy and workforce over the past generation. For example, service-sector employment has continued to grow—to the point where it now accounts for 80 percent of employment—in contrast to goods production in such areas as manufacturing, mining, construction, and agriculture.[3] In other words, four-fifths of working Americans now provide services—wholesale and retail trade, finance, insurance and real estate, personal services, government, and so on—instead of producing tangible goods for a living.

And blue-collar work has continued to decline throughout this time period. At this point, blue-collar workers (laborers as well as craft, operative, and transportation workers) make up only about 25 percent of the workforce, compared to 58 percent who are white-collar (managers, professionals, technicians, salespeople, and clerical workers).[4] There are more people working in doctors' offices than in auto plants, more in laundries and dry cleaners than in steel mills.[5]

There are also many more women in the paid labor force. Having risen fully 50 percent from the early 1970s, the rate of women working away from home in America is now one of the very highest in the world. More than 70 percent of mothers with children ranging in age from six to seventeen now work outside the home, as do more than 50 percent of women with children aged one year or less.[6]

The economy is also more international than it once was. The summed value of U.S. imports and exports is now about a quarter of our gross domestic product (GDP), twice that of a generation ago, meaning that the U.S. economy is more and more intertwined with economies abroad. The growth in international financial flows greatly accentuates this interdependence. Worldwide, the *daily* volume of currency trading has grown from slightly over $50 billion in the mid-1980s to about $1.5 trillion today.[7]

The use of computers on the job has also exploded. When it was first measured by the Bureau of the Census's Current Population Survey (CPS) in 1984, about 20 percent of the workforce used computers. Now about half do—a huge shift in a short period of time.[8] And the influence and use of the Internet continues its meteoric rise in this, the world's most wired nation.

But while in these ways and others we may indeed have a "new" economy, for most participants—and we have the highest rate of labor-force participation in the world—an old problem has persisted: finding work that adequately supports people and their families. Given our stingy welfare state, how well Americans live depends—more than in any other developed country—on their pay and benefits at work. And for many working Americans, the new economy, until very recently, has unfortunately been more new than good.

The Great Slowdown and Growing Apart

Though it's hard to remember this in the current economic boom, a substantial drop in U.S. economic growth, and an even sharper drop in productivity growth, occurred between 1973 and 1999—a set of historic changes best described by journalist Jeffrey Madrick in his book, *The End of Affluence*.[9] We call this change the "Great Slowdown." As shown in Chart 1.1, economic growth was almost 4 percent a year in the 1947–73 postwar period, but it dropped to just 3 percent in the rest of the 1970s, a rate that continued throughout the 1980s and 1990s. Productivity growth, the rate at which output per hour worked goes up—of even greater consequence for living standards—suddenly dropped from 3 percent a year before 1973 to less than half that level in the 1970s, barely improved in the 1980s (to 1.4 percent),

CHART 1.1   Real GDP and Productivity Growth, 1947–99

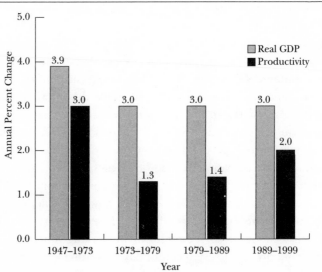

Sources: Authors' analysis of Bureau of Economic Analysis and Bureau of Labor Statistics data; Dean Baker, "What's New in the Nineties? An Analysis of Economic Performance in the Nineties Business Cycle," in Jeff Madrick, ed., *Perspectives on Economics* (New York: The Century Foundation, forthcoming).

and then recovered more substantially (to 2.0 percent) in the 1990s. But even with the 1990s improvement, productivity growth for that decade remained a full percentage point below its rapid pace in the 1947–73 era.

This steep drop in growth of output and productivity necessarily meant a slowdown in wage (and income) growth, since productivity gains generally set an upper bound on wage gains. So the Great Slowdown would have meant a substantial cut in living standards growth no matter what. For example, if wage and income gains were 2 or 3 percent a year before 1973, we would have expected, all else being equal, that they had subsided to about half that after 1973.

Consider the income trajectory of the typical forgotten majority household under this scenario. Such a household in 1973 probably had an income of around $34,000,[10] making it more than twice as well-off as the equivalent household in 1947. Even with the slower productivity growth in the post-1973 period, that typical forgotten majority household should still have gotten half again as rich in this period, putting it over $50,000 by the late 1990s.

But all else, it turns out, was not equal. In the post-1973 period, in contrast to the pre-1973 period, some did rather well while many did amazingly poorly. This is our second big change—"Growing Apart"—by which we mean the tremendous rise in economic inequality in America since the 1970s. This rise in inequality meant that the members of the typical forgotten majority household did not begin to realize the gains that should have been theirs even in a world of slower growth. On the contrary, their economic situation barely budged after 1973, while their college-educated counterparts continued to advance.

We believe that the degree to which the benefits of growth and productivity are widely shared is a basic measure of economic performance in a democracy—and, further, that such widely shared benefits help generate positive feelings about a society and its government. In these terms, the U.S. economy performed superbly for the first three decades after World War II. The rising tide of postwar prosperity really did "lift all boats," as President Kennedy used to like to say. Indeed, as Chart 1.2 indicates, boats at the bottom actually rose a little faster than those at the top. But since the early 1970s, especially in the two decades since 1979, the gap between rich and poor has grown steadily. National income and wealth, of course, have continued to grow, but because of this rising inequality, only the top 20 percent have really made significant gains. And the bottom 60 percent, as the chart shows, have barely budged, ranging from very modest gains to actual income losses over the time period.

CHART 1.2   Family Income: Average Annual Change, 1947–49

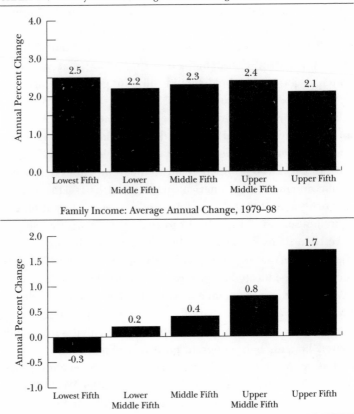

Family Income: Average Annual Change, 1979–98

Source: Economic Policy Institute analysis of Bureau of the Census data, 1947–98.

The Great Divide

During this period of rising income inequality, the value of a four-year college degree has dramatically increased. Those with a B.A. or B.S. from a four-year college have continued to move ahead; those without it have fallen farther and farther behind. For example, between 1979 and 1999,[11] the average real hourly wage for those with a college degree[12] went up 14 percent; and for those with advanced degrees, 19 percent. In contrast, average wages[13] for those with only some college fell 4 percent; for those with a high school diploma, 10 percent; and for high school dropouts, a stunning 24 percent. Men among the latter three groups did even worse: They were down 7, 15, and 27 percent, respectively.[14]

The difference in outcome for those with "full college" degrees and those without is big enough to warrant its own name. Let's call it the "Great Divide." Almost three-quarters of the American workforce stand on one side of this divide, lacking a college degree, and for them the "new economy" has, until very recently, delivered only modest gains, usually purchased at the price of increased family work hours. For example, from 1973 to 1998, in an economy that almost doubled in real terms, the wage of the typical worker in production and nonsupervisory jobs (80 percent of the workforce)[15] actually *declined* by 6 percent, from $13.61 to $12.77 an hour. Based on a forty-hour week, this works out to a loss of about $1,750 a year for the typical worker. Without a compensating action like a spouse working more hours, such circumstances could make a real dent in a family's food budget, not to mention some of those "extras" like vacations that are central to a middle-class lifestyle. That loss compares to wage gains of 79 percent for the typical worker between 1947 and 1973, as his or her hourly wage rose all the way from $7.61 to $12.77.[16] Figured on the same basis, the average worker gained $10,750 a year over this period—a huge boost to family economic fortunes.

As we would expect from these wage trends, the income of the typical (median) family basically flattened out after 1973, rising only 12 percent over the twenty-five-year period between 1973 and 1998, compared to 104 percent—that is, more than doubled—over the twenty-six years between 1947 and 1973. This amazing failure of slow growth to deliver even commensurately modest gains can be seen at a glance in Chart 1.3.

CHART 1.3   Growth in GDP Versus Family Income and Hourly Wage, 1947–98

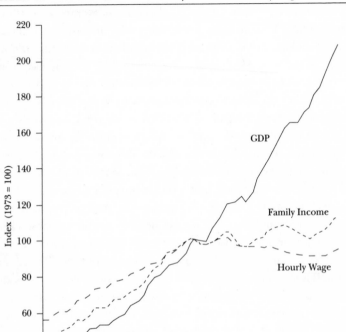

Source: Economic Policy Institute analysis of Bureau of Economic Analysis, Bureau of the Census, and Bureau of Labor Statistics data, 1947–98.

What this meant concretely was that the typical blue-collar or low-level white-collar worker was on a rapid escalator to the middle class until 1973, but after that had to work hard simply to maintain his or her hold on the income necessary to maintain a middle-class lifestyle. The rapid escalator bred a sense of confidence and security; the subsequent stagnation bred uncertainty and insecurity.

These trends highlight the continued presence of class concerns in the new economy. People are indeed increasingly working in the service sector, in white-collar jobs, and, above all, with computers. In that sense, more and more workers are part of the "new economy," and many may even qualify as "wired workers." But for those on the other side of the Great Divide—including many of the very same wired workers—all these changes have meant little in terms of concrete economic progress.

Defining the White Working Class

It is this Great Divide that defines the new white working class.[17] On one side of the Great Divide, lacking a four-year college degree, are the vast majority—three-quarters—of white adults who have not fared well over the last quarter-century. On the other side are the quarter of white adults who have a four-year degree or more and for whom the last twenty-five years have been a time of substantial economic progress.

Of course, these non-college-educated whites are "not your father's" white working class. Instead of blue-collar work, this new white working class is more likely to be doing low-level white-collar and service work. And instead of working in manufacturing, the new white working class is much more likely to be working in an office with a computer or at a similar service-sector job. The members of this group are also likely to have more education—perhaps a few years in college, maybe even an A.A. degree—and those in the workforce are much more likely to be female. *But, in economic terms, they are not so different from the white working class of previous generations.*

These voters are the real "swing" in American politics. Their loyalties shift the most from election to election and, in so doing, determine the winners in American politics. They are also the majority—about 55 percent of voters and of the adult population.[18] But they don't receive much attention these days; they are invisible to the journalists and commentators who define our national discourse. To bring them into focus more sharply, we now review some basic information about them. As we proceed, it will become clear that the new white working class is quite at variance with dated stereotypes from the 1970s and 1980s.

1. THE DAYS OF HIGH SCHOOL DROPOUTS ARE LONG GONE. More than four-fifths of the forgotten majority have at least a high school diploma. Almost two-fifths have some education beyond high school, with about 10 percent holding an associate degree.[19] Note, however, that the economic situation of those with an associate degree is very similar to the economic situation of those with some college but no degree: The median household income of whites with an associate degree is about $54,000, compared to about $51,000 among whites with some college only.[20]

2. THEY EARN A MODERATE INCOME. The forgotten majority's median household income is about $42,000, a figure on the low side of what is generally considered a middle class income.[21] About two-thirds have household incomes between $15,000 and $75,000. About one-seventh are below that range, about one-fifth above it.[22]

3. THEY ARE MOSTLY LOW-LEVEL WHITE-COLLAR AND SERVICE WORKERS, NOT UNSKILLED BLUE-COLLAR WORKERS. As might be expected, more than 80 percent of the forgotten majority works outside of professional-managerial jobs.[23] Moreover, even those forgotten majority workers who do have professional or managerial positions tend to hold relatively low-level, poorly paid jobs. For example, white managers with a college degree average

$71,000 in earnings, compared to white managers with some college who average only $45,000 in earnings and white managers with a high school diploma who only average $39,000.[24]

More surprising, perhaps, is that the bulk of forgotten majority jobs are not blue-collar, but rather in low-level white collar (technical, sales, clerical) and service occupations. The few blue collar jobs that remain are increasingly likely to be skilled positions: only 17 percent of forgotten majority workers currently hold unskilled blue-collar jobs (even among forgotten majority *men*, the figure is less than one-quarter).

4. THEY ARE LESS AND LESS LIKELY TO WORK IN FACTORY JOBS. Today, only a relatively small proportion (17 percent) of the forgotten majority works in manufacturing (even among men, the proportion is less than one-quarter). In fact, the entire goods-producing sector, which includes construction, mining, and agriculture, as well as manufacturing, employs only three in ten forgotten majority workers. This leaves the overwhelming majority—seven in ten—within the service sector, including government. There are almost as many members of the new white working class working in trade alone (especially retail) as there are in all goods-producing jobs.

5. THEY LIVE IN—AND DOMINATE—THE SUBURBS. The forgotten majority is underrepresented in our urban areas (totaling just over one-third of adults) and overrepresented in our rapidly dwindling rural ones (totaling almost three-quarters of adults). But in the growing suburbs,[25] generally viewed as the current battleground of American politics, it represents almost three-fifths of adults. In contrast, college-educated whites number just over one-fifth of suburban adults.

The conventional view of the suburban electorate—affluent soccer moms, executive dads, and so on—is drawn from wealthy suburban towns like Bethesda (Maryland) and Fairlawn (New Jersey), and it doesn't come close to presenting an accurate picture. The suburban electorate is in fact composed mostly of members of the forgotten majority: two-earner families of low to moderate education and income, generally working in low-level white-collar, service, and skilled blue-collar jobs.

In sum, the white working class remains numerically dominant, even if its form has changed. Sure, many of its members qualify as wired workers, in the narrow sense that they work with computers and information technology. Many also qualify as soccer moms, in the narrow sense that they are working women who have to juggle work and family, including driving their kids around town to athletic contests. And certainly many qualify as suburban independents, in the narrow sense that they live in the suburbs and lack a strong identification with either party. But they remain members of a new white working class whose economic interests and experience diverge fundamentally from soccer moms in Bethesda, suburban independents in Fairlawn, and wired cyber-professionals in Silicon Valley.

The Forgotten Majority's Values

It's clear that the economic interests and experience of the forgotten majority set it apart from its more educated and affluent counterparts. But what about values? It's a truism in politics that values matter; some even claim, as Ben Wattenberg did in his 1995 book, that "values matter most."[26]

It's certainly difficult to deny that people vote on a broader basis than economic issues and experience. And even in terms of economic issues and experience, people's values inevitably influence how they view their experience and evaluate policy ideas; otherwise, how would they make sense of that experience and prioritize what they want? But this is not to say that voting is therefore all about values. Rather, the point is that values are always a *part* of voting, and that separating values from economics in political decisions is an intrinsically difficult, and somewhat arbitrary, exercise. In other words, it's more correct to say "values always matter" than "values matter most."

So, rather than emphasizing an artificial distinction between values voting and economic voting, we wish to focus on the *relationship* between values and economics in voting. In particular, we believe that a disjuncture between economic experience and values has fundamentally shaped the political behavior of the forgotten majority. The economic experience has already been described; the values we have in mind are deeply held and broadly shared ones about opportunity, fair reward for effort, the centrality of hard work and individual achievement, and social commitment. In the last quarter-century, these values have been repeatedly contradicted and called into question by the tremendous slowdown—and reversal, for some—in the escalator to the middle class we described earlier. The failure of activist government to restart that escalator, combined with its apparent concentration on the problems or rights of others[27] (minorities, the poor, gays, even criminals), convinced forgotten majority voters that government was more part of this values-experience disjuncture than its solution. The direct result is the sour and skeptical attitude toward government we still see today.

Of course, the forgotten majority has a diversity of values beyond the broadly shared ones just mentioned, and the latter sometimes enter into political decisions. For example, attitudes toward abortion and homosexuality are often related to religious beliefs and consequently vary widely across the forgotten majority. A full description or model of forgotten majority voting behavior would thus have to take these values and others, and their varying influences, into account.

However, we don't seek to develop such a full model in this volume. Rather, our purpose is to show how important the relationship between values and economics is to the political behavior of the forgotten majority and how incomplete and misleading the story is when that relationship is left out.

America's Forgotten Majority and Our Future

The role of the forgotten majority is also key to understanding the potential of current strategies being pursued by the Democratic, Republican, and Reform parties. The ideal strategy, in our view, is one that recognizes the centrality of the forgotten majority and seeks to *reunite* the values of these voters with their economic experience—in other words, to heal the disjuncture that has marked the post-1973 period. The political party that is able to do this should have the inside track on the long-term loyalty of these voters and therefore, potentially, the base for a dominant coalition.

This is a favorable time to pursue the project of reuniting the forgotten majority's values with its economic experience. The last several years have been a period of fast economic growth, with low unemployment, rapidly rising real wages, and a slowing down and, in some cases, reversal of the trend toward greater inequality. In other words, work is being rewarded in a way that just hasn't been seen for a generation or so, taking the edge off the forgotten majority's suspicion of government and the political parties. In addition, there is less conflict around issues like abortion and homosexuality to detract from such an effort. America has become, in many ways, a very tolerant society in which intolerance itself is quite unpopular. This makes it easier to focus on values that members of the forgotten majority share among themselves and with other voters, as opposed to values that keep them apart.

With that in mind, how are the major parties and their major alternative—the Reform party—doing? Democratic party strategy suffers from a refusal to recognize the forgotten majority as key to its drive to build a new popular majority, despite the party's continued poor performance among these voters. Instead, the Democratic party prefers to target various fashionable voter groups—from soccer moms to wired voters to suburban independents—as a supplement to its union/minority base, and hope it manages to outpoll the GOP as it did in the last two presidential elections.

The Democratic party also lacks a program to unite the values and economic experience of the forgotten majority, beyond hoping that the current expansion lasts forever, which history suggests is unlikely. Even now, that expansion is doing little to solve long-term problems like health security, retirement security, and education reform that are crucial to the forgotten majority's economic future. These problems demand bold policy interventions—interventions that the Democrats are reluctant to propose, given their born-again commitment to fiscal prudence and modest government. But without such initiatives, forgotten majority voters are unlikely to see the Democratic program as the bridge between their values and the economic future they desire.

The GOP is similarly reluctant to recognize the centrality of the forgotten majority, despite the fact that—as we shall see—its electoral successes have been dependent on support from this group. It has also had difficulty articulating a program that could reunite the forgotten majority's values with its economic experience. Indeed, the GOP remains wedded to an anti-tax and anti-government rhetoric that is out of step with the forgotten majority and fails to provide a compelling vision for this group's economic future.

Finally, the Reform party at least has the advantage of recognizing its target. As we shall see, the Reform party has been primarily an electoral vehicle for a segment of the forgotten majority, and there is every indication that the party continues to appreciate this fact. The problem—besides the generic difficulty of being a third party in a system that favors two major parties—is that the Reform party's social values are out of synch with those of most forgotten majority voters (either too conservative or too libertarian, depending on the faction) and its economic program does not go much beyond railing against corporate power and globalization. The forgotten majority is sympathetic to such a critique—as the Seattle protests of late 1999 strongly suggest—but more interested in an approach that deals with its economic problems as a whole and can provide solutions in synch with its values. For most forgotten majority voters, anxieties about globalization just don't translate into the kind of protectionism that the Reform party advocates.

So no party—Democrat, Republican, or Reform—really is on course to embrace the forgotten majority and its concerns, heal the wounds of the last generation, and reap the consequent electoral rewards. Granted, there have been positive signs—Republicans becoming more compassionate and less rigidly antigovernment, Democrats becoming more willing to propose new spending on key problems like health care and education—that suggest new approaches more in keeping with this goal. But what remains to be seen is how the forgotten majority will react to these fairly cautious departures.

In short, politics in the early 21st century is very much up for grabs. The members of the forgotten majority, the real swing voters in politics today, are waiting for someone who really understands both their values *and* their economic experience. Right now, that could come from any political direction, and which direction it comes from will determine the shape of government in the early 21st century.

TWO

How the Forgotten Majority Enriches the Conventional Wisdom on U.S. Politics

The New Economy favors a rising Learning Class over a declining working class . . . a new Learning Class of workers who will
dominate at least the first half of the 21st century. They will be
better-educated, more affluent, more mobile, and more self-re-
liant. They are less likely to be influenced by (let alone submit
to) large mediating institutions. Their political outlook and behavior will increasingly defy the class-based divisions of the old
economy.

—WILLIAM GALSTON AND ELAINE KAMARCK FOR
THE DEMOCRATIC LEADERSHIP COUNCIL, FALL 1998[1]

IN PARTISAN TERMS, the big thing that's happened in American electoral politics in the last several decades is a major shift
away from the Democratic party. After controlling the House, the
Senate, and most state legislatures and governor's mansions al-

most continuously since the New Deal, Democrats have lost their majorities in all of these branches of government. And where—as with Bill Clinton's presidency—they've gotten something back in the 1990s, their base of support has been thin and unreliable. Moreover, Democratic politics, particularly at the presidential level, now bears uncanny similarities to that of centrist Republicans of old. In policy terms, measured against the commitments to activist government and equality that marked the New Deal and Great Society, there's no question that, over the past generation, American politics has taken a very substantial turn to the right.

In the first chapter we suggested that the popular base for this move to the right should be located among voters of the forgotten majority. But other demographic interpretations of the origins of today's politics also deserve consideration. Indeed, these other interpretations—focused on demographic shifts toward the suburbs, toward white-collar work, and toward use of information technology on the job—form a critical part of the conventional wisdom on today's politics and, as such, typically get more attention than the forgotten majority–based explanation we favor.

Have Demographic Shifts Caused the Move to the Right?

The argument here runs as follows. Suburban (or white-collar or "new economy") voters are understood, more or less by their very nature, to be less interested in government activism than urban (or blue-collar or "old economy") voters. It follows that as a larger and larger share of the electorate comes to occupy these intrinsically conservative voting camps, the electorate as a whole becomes more conservative.

Like much that passes for conventional wisdom, the reliance on structural changes as an overarching explanation is not supported by convincing evidence. As we show below, a review of the relevant data matches up only poorly with observed political changes such as the decline in the Democratic share of the presidential vote since 1960 and the rise of key "conservative" voter attitudes (e.g., distrust of government).

Suburbanization

Suburbanization is perhaps the most popular of all demographic[2] explanations, and also the least scrutinized. The suburbanization of America and the image of the conservative, tax-fearing suburban voter are firmly implanted in the popular consciousness, giving the explanation good surface plausibility to most people. But when you look below the surface, does the explanation hold up?

We see substantial political effects from demographic changes when two requirements are met—that is, when (1) the magnitude of that change is fairly large (e.g., a lot of people have to move to suburbia) and (2) the change has to involve the movement of people who have substantially different political views or behaviors (e.g., suburbanites have to vote and think really differently from people who live elsewhere).[3] One without the other generally won't work. For example, a tiny shift between two categories—say, between blacks and whites—even where there are big political differences between them, won't affect politics much. Nor will a large shift between two categories that act almost the same politically.

Suburbanization flunks the second test. That is, while a fairly large shift toward the suburbs has occurred over time—an increase of about 19 percentage points in the 1960–96 period[4]—the net shift has *not* been between categories of voters with strong political differences. When most people think of suburbanization—and this is part of what gives the theory surface plausibility—they think of people leaving cities, whose residents are notoriously more liberal than suburbanites. Looking at the country as a whole, however, suburban growth came not from urban populations but from rural ones.

Over the nearly forty-year period from 1960 to 1996, as many northern cities emptied out, southern and western cities grew. The net decline in the urban population was, as a result, a mere 2 percent. What really declined during this period was the share of the population in rural areas—down 17 percent. The move from rural areas to suburbs would cancel out any "suburbanization" effect, since rural and suburban voters tend to act similarly, particularly once we factor in other demographic characteristics such as race, education, and income. While one more conservative voting group increased in size, another shrunk by about the same amount.

A simple statistical procedure known as shift-share analysis confirms this interpretation.[5] The procedure shows that if the Democratic vote in urban, suburban, and rural areas had remained exactly as it was in 1960–64 (the Kennedy-Johnson elections), but the distribution of voters between these areas had shifted just as it did between 1960–64 and 1992–96 (the Clinton elections), the Democratic share of the popular vote for president would have dropped only four-tenths of a percentage point, compared to the actual drop of 9.3 points. This indicates that suburbanization, by itself, can account for only a very small part (4 percent) of the drop in the Democratic presidential vote over the last three decades. A similar calculation shows that suburbanization accounts for *none* of the massive increase[6] (47 percentage points) in distrust of government over the same time period. Other calculations performed on other attitudes toward government have yielded similar results.

The conclusion is as clear as it is counterintuitive: *Suburbanization, by itself, has very little to do with the changed political climate we live in today.* For a satisfactory explanation, we must turn elsewhere.

"White-Collarization"

Another explanation concerns the shift toward white-collar jobs since the 1960s. White-collar workers are generally believed to be more conservative on economics than blue-collar workers, who historically formed the bedrock of the New Deal coalition. This relative conservatism is attributed to, among other things, less income insecurity, more satisfying work, and higher status.[7] Therefore, since the weight of these workers in the population has obviously increased, the argument goes, it might be the reason for the declining support for activist government and the Democratic party.

Though definitions of what constitutes blue- and white-collar work vary, most data sources confirm a significant shift from blue- to white-collar work over the last thirty years. In particular, a fairly large shift occurred in the percentage of so-called high white-collar workers, those who occupy professional-managerial[8] positions, between the early 1960s and the 1990s. Since these workers exhibited relatively low support levels for the Democrats (and still do so), they are a likely source of weakened support for the Democrats.

Statistical estimates[9] confirm that "white-collarization" has been a contributing factor to weakened Democratic support. However, the magnitude of this contribution is still relatively small, explaining an estimated 14 percent of the decline in average Democratic presidential support between the Kennedy-Johnson and Clinton elections. And this estimate is probably too high, since our data source here (the National Election Studies) overestimates the magnitude of the shift to white-collar work quite substantially when compared with official government data.[10]

White-collarization fares even worse as an explanation for rising distrust of government. Similar statistical calculations show that the effect of the shift toward white-collar work should have been to *reduce* distrust of government slightly, by a couple of percentage points. This is because, on average, white-collar workers are slightly more trusting of government than blue-collar workers. Again, it appears that we must look farther afield for a satisfactory explanation of today's political climate.

"Wired Workers"

A related and increasingly popular demographic story about American politics is based on the concept that the new information-based economy is transforming jobs, producing legions of "wired workers" whose take on politics is fundamentally different from that of "old economy" workers.[11] These wired voters, it is argued, are fundamentally libertarian; are hostile to traditional activist policies, which they view as bureaucratic; favor only a limited government role for programs like training vouchers; and generally want government to get out of the way so that information technology can transform the world.

To the extent this story is true, it certainly might help explain weak support for activist government and an activist Democratic party. The work of economist Stephen Rose[12] allows us to test this theory directly, since Rose has carefully analyzed changes in the job structure over the last several decades and developed a typology of job functions that maps the outlines of the emerging "new" economy. We can apply this typology to recent National Election Studies data to see whether wired workers are politically different in the way predicted.

As Chart 2.1 shows, the key change in the job structure over the last thirty-five years, according to Rose's typology, has been the decline of industrial production (the "Factory" function in his terminology) and the rise of management, administrative, business, and financial services (the "Office" function). While each function used to account for about one-third of employment, the Office now accounts for more than two-fifths and the

CHART 2.1 Distribution of Employment by Occupation/Industry Category

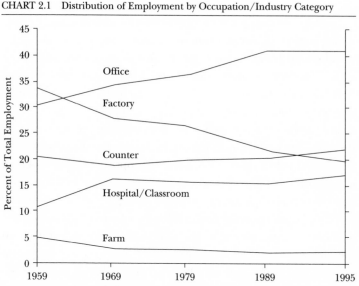

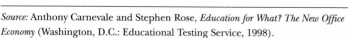

Source: Anthony Carnevale and Stephen Rose, *Education for What? The New Office Economy* (Washington, D.C.: Educational Testing Service, 1998).

Factory accounts for less than one-fifth. Clearly, this is a change of substantial magnitude, reflecting the emergence of the new economy as we are coming to know it.

But exactly who are these office workers who now dominate the job structure of the economy? As defined by Rose, there are five subgroups: (1) managers[13] involved in coordinating and supervising activities in industries, producing goods, or performing services; (2) employees in the entire finance, insurance, and real estate (FIRE) sector; (3) business professionals employed in the managerial hierarchy, mostly accountants, sales representatives, and the like; (4) employees in public administration and non-profit social service institutions; and (5) support staff, primarily clerical and administrative. As the preceding list suggests, these office workers are distinguished less by their mastery and use of new technologies than by their function in administering and coordinating today's complex economy. Indeed, the group whose involvement with new technologies is most pronounced (and whose education levels are the highest) is the high-skilled services group (the "Hospital/Classroom" function), which accounts for less than one-fifth of total employment in Rose's typology.

And, as it turns out, office workers are not distinguished by their low levels of support for the Democrats or their hostility to government.[14] In 1996, office workers supported the Democratic presidential candidate at a rate of just under the national average (48 versus 49 percent), while the group linked most directly to new technologies, the high-skill services sector, supported the Democratic candidate at a rate 6 percentage points higher than the national average. And, counterintuitively, the one group whose Democratic support rate was notably lower than the national average was the Factory sector, hardly the cutting edge of the new economy.[15] Finally, there are no statistically significant differences among these five categories in terms of level of trust of national government. All of these findings suggest that the rise of wired workers and the new economy do not have the political effects generally assumed.

We can further underscore these findings by breaking down the Office category into the five subcategories mentioned above. The data show a spread of support levels for the Democrats, including one subcategory (the FIRE sector) where support for Clinton was 9 points lower than the national level and another subcategory (the clerical-administrative sector) where support was 11 points higher than the national average). This suggests that the leading edge of the new economy, the burgeoning Office function, simultaneously creates jobs that disadvantage and advantage the Democrats and activist government. For every new wired professional trolling cyberspace there's at least one new low-level worker doing mundane clerical/administrative tasks. Both the professional and the low-level worker use computers, but their interests, economic experience, and outlook on the world are probably quite different.

Summing all this up: The precise net effect of the growth of the "new" economy on support for activist government, though unclear, should certainly not be assumed to be heavily negative. Thus, this last demographic shift also falls short as an explanation for the contemporary political climate.

America's Forgotten Majority: The Real Demographic Story

As shall see, the real demographic story doesn't lie in shifts but, rather, in change *within* the key demographic of the forgotten majority. Consider first the data presented in Table 2.1. These data show that the drop in Democratic presidential support has occurred entirely among whites, by 13 percentage points over the entire 1960–64 to 1992–96 time period, and by an even sharper 18 or 19 points when we compare the Kennedy-Johnson elections (1960–64) to either the Nixon elections (1968–72) or the Reagan elections (1980–84).

Table 2.2 further shows that almost all of the decline in Democratic presidential support among whites between the Kennedy-Johnson and Clinton elections occurred among the forgotten majority, defined as whites without a four-year college degree. The decline in that group was a sharp 14 percentage points. Among college-educated whites, on the other hand, the Democratic vote was nearly flat—down a mere percentage point over the same time period.

The basic pattern also holds when we compare the Kennedy-Johnson elections to the Democratic nadirs of the Nixon and Reagan elections (i.e., when these candidates averaged 40 and 41

TABLE 2.1 Democratic Presidential Vote: Whites Versus Blacks, 1960–96 (in percentages)

	Whites	Blacks
1960–64	53.1	88.4
1968–72	34.7	92.0
1980–94	34.2	91.7
1992–96	39.7	92.6
Change: 1960–64 to 1992–96	−13.4	4.2

Source: Authors' analysis of National Election Studies data, 1960–96.

TABLE 2.2 Democratic Presidential Vote Among Whites: College-Educated Versus Forgotten Majority, 1960–96 (in percentages)

	1960–64	1968–72	1980–84	1992–96	Change: 1960–64 to 1992–96
Forgotten Majority					
All	55.0	34.6	34.5	40.8	−14.2
Men	56.7	30.9	32.2	36.1	−20.6
Women	53.6	37.4	36.2	44.5	−8.9
College-Educated Whites					
All	39.1	35.7	33.1	38.1	−1.0
Men	36.7	35.5	29.3	31.8	−4.9
Women	41.9	35.9	37.0	46.1	4.2

Source: Authors' analysis of National Election Studies data, 1960–96.

percent of the popular vote, respectively). In both cases, the drop-off (compared to 1960–64) was an astonishing 20 percentage points among forgotten majority voters, compared to relatively trivial declines of 3 and 6 percentage points among college-educated whites. (Note that this decline in forgotten majority support was not concentrated in the South, contrary to the claims of some analysts; indeed, it was steep in every region of the country.)

Another striking outcome revealed in Table 2.2 is the differences between men and women of varying levels of education. Forgotten majority women show a healthy decline in Democratic support of 9 points between the Kennedy-Johnson and Clinton elections, but forgotten majority *men* display a much larger drop of 21 points over the same period. Again, the pattern continues when we compare the Kennedy-Johnson elections to the Nixon and Reagan elections: much larger drops among men (26 and 25 percentage points, respectively) than among women (17 and 18 points, respectively). Also note that Democrat support trends among *college-educated* whites show a similar pattern of gender differences: Democratic support among college-educated white men declined by 5 points between the Kennedy-Johnson and Clinton elections but actually *increased* by 4 points among their female counterparts.

Since members of the forgotten majority differ significantly in their levels of education, ranging from high school dropouts to those who not only completed high school but also pursued college-level studies and perhaps even attained an associate degree, it is worth asking how Democratic decline has been distributed *within* the white working class.

Such analysis reveals two interesting findings that shed additional light on the Democratic drop-off among the forgotten majority. First, between the Kennedy-Johnson and Clinton elections, this decline was sharpest (15 percentage points) among those with a high school diploma but no further education and least sharp among those with some college (down 4 points). Thus, white high school graduates appear to have been a particular trouble spot for Democrats.

Second, a large shift in the educational credentials of forgotten majority voters occurred over this time period, such that the proportion of high school dropout voters, among whom Democratic support was fairly high in the early 1960s, declined drastically (by about three-quarters), while the proportion of voters with some college,[16] among whom Democratic support was low to begin with, almost doubled.[17] Statistical analyses[18] suggest that about one-third of the Democratic drop-off in support among the forgotten majority can be attributed to this shift away from high school dropouts toward those with some college. Thus, another great weakness of the Democrats with respect to the new white working class has been *a failure to increase their support among a burgeoning voter group—those with some college—where they have never been strong.*

In these two events—the precipitous decline in support among high school–educated whites and the continued poor (and worsening) performance among whites with some college—we see the two basic factors behind declining Democratic presidential support among the forgotten majority. It is these changes—changes within the forgotten majority demographic—that actually provided the popular base for the move to the right over the last generation, not demographic shifts like suburbanization and the rise of white-collar work.

This leads to our next question: What prompted forgotten majority voters to turn away from the Democrats and activist government? In the first chapter, we suggested that a disjuncture between their core values and economic experience led them to judge government's efficacy and priorities harshly. But other broad, society-wide changes in the last several decades may have pushed the forgotten majority in the same direction. These deserve a hearing.

Have the Values of Americans Become More Conservative?

One possibility is that most Americans' values have simply become more conservative over time and the forgotten majority is responding politically to these changes. If so, a consideration of their economic experience is unnecessary to an understanding of their evolution toward conservatism.

Consistent with value-change theory, politicians of both parties spend more time than they used to talking about values and proclaiming the centrality of good values to their politics. Perhaps this hyperresponsiveness to values reflects a shift to the right with which all politicians must contend. If so, it would help explain the unfavorable climate for the Democrats and activist government in the 1990s, since Republicans have been more effective in positioning themselves as defenders of conservative values.

In spite of this theory's popularity, there's really no evidence for it. There is a substantial core of key American values that are relevant to the evaluation of policy—but these have changed very little since the 1960s. And what change has taken place has been directly counter to what the theory assumes. Even as policy has shifted to the right on many issues, the American electorate has become more, not less, liberal.

Let's start with the core values. What are they? Pollster Daniel Yankelovich,[19] based on his review of six decades of survey data archived at the University of Connecticut's Roper Center, has found that the American public consistently and overwhelmingly endorses the following values: freedom, equality before the law, equality of opportunity, fairness (a belief that people should be fairly rewarded for their efforts), achievement and hard work (a belief in the efficacy of individual effort), patriotism, democracy, American exceptionalism (a belief in the special moral status of the United States), caring beyond the self, religion, and luck. This is quite a substantial list of very politically relevant values. Indeed, values like opportunity, fairness, individual achievement, and caring beyond the self seem to lie at the very heart of contemporary political debate. Yet there is little evidence that any more or less of the public endorses these values now than at the beginning of the 1960s. For example, polling data collected over forty-five years show that 70 percent or more of the public endorse the centrality of hard work to getting ahead and achieving one's goals.[20]

So what *has* changed in the values realm? The answer points to perhaps the biggest surprise of all. Exhaustive studies of public opinion suggest that most of the movement in the realm of values (as opposed to views about policy)[21] in the last several decades has occurred in a *liberal*, not conservative, direction.[22] Yankelovich gives several examples of these liberal shifts: less value placed on social conformity, greater acceptance of lifestyle diversity, more value placed on individual expressiveness, more value placed on respecting the environment, less rigid rules about sexuality, less puritanism about pleasure, greater acceptance of alternative family forms, belief in more equal relationships and shared responsibilities between men and women, and general support for women's rights. To cite just one example, 40 percent of the public in 1969 (75 percent in 1938!) disapproved of a married woman working if she had a husband capable of supporting her, compared to just 19 percent in 1988.[23] Of course, there have been ups and downs in the level of public support for these values; but it seems hard to deny that, considered over a several-decade time frame, the shift in these values has occurred in a decisively liberal direction.

So a set of core, politically central values has not changed over time, while another set of values—generally in the areas of social tolerance, the environment, individual expression, and women's rights—has moved in a generally liberal direction. This finding makes value change seem a poor candidate for explaining changing attitudes toward the Democratic party and activist government. Indeed, sociologist Clem Brooks[24] provides strong evidence that increasing liberalism around the role of women in society[25] has played a substantial role in *propping up* Democratic support levels in a Republican era. Similarly, the failure of the Monica Lewinsky scandal to erode Democratic support is another piece of evidence that value change in a liberal direction—in this case, greater tolerance of sexual misbehavior, and a willingness to separate private failings from public performance—is actually helping the Democrats weather problems that might have been fatal several decades ago. Can anyone imagine a president getting caught having oral sex in the Oval Office in 1970 and not being tossed out at the first opportunity?

There is, however, one school of thought that attempts to connect these value changes to a sea change in politics consistent with declining support for activist government—namely, the "postmaterialist" perspective on value change. Pioneered by political scientist Ronald Inglehart in the early 1970s,[26] this argument contends that there are two kinds of values: materialist (centered on economic and physical security) and postmaterialist (centered on freedom, self-expression, and quality of life). As society has advanced materially, many more people can take their economic and physical security roughly for granted, leaving more time to focus on the postmaterialist values. Politics has consequently changed, since political conflict now centers on building freedom, self-expression, and quality of life, rather than on using the state to improve citizens' material welfare.

It's hard to argue that these "postmaterialist" values are not broadly embraced in the United States today. Much of the evidence just offered on social tolerance, for example, shows that they are. What *can* be argued about is the idea that such values are now more important than materialist values and that this value shift explains contemporary politics. First, in 1973, the long postwar economic boom ended, and America embarked on a generation of economic experience anomalous in our history—a period of prolonged income stagnation and wage decline. Therefore, the emergence of postmaterialist values, driven by increasing material affluence, is a poor candidate for explaining post-1973 political changes. Second, Inglehart's basic evidence for asserting the growing dominance of postmaterialist values is deeply flawed. His evidence is based almost entirely on forcing people to decide what are the most and second-most important goals among these four choices: (1) fighting rising prices, (2) maintaining order in the nation, (3) giving the people more say in important government decisions, and (4) protecting freedom of speech. As sociologist James Davis[27] points out, this is not a convincing way of assessing the changing balance between economic and noneconomic concerns. What is touted as a clean materialist versus postmaterialist set of questions (choices 1 and 2 versus choices 3 and 4) is really three items about authoritarianism plus one narrow economic item about inflation. Thus, what the questions really measure over time, independent of feelings about inflation, is an unsurprising shift toward anti-authoritarianism. Any broader statements about postmaterialist values and the rise of anti-statist politics are simply not justified by Inglehart's work—or, for that matter, by that of others, which also shows that clearer measures of postmaterialism don't explain the rise of anti-statist politics.[28]

So we are back to a mismatch between the value change that has actually taken place—mostly liberal—and the political changes we are trying to explain. Does this mean we should therefore jettison values *per se* as an explanatory factor in political change over the last several decades? No, it simply means we should jettison value *change* as an important factor. Values themselves—specifically, the core values around opportunity, fairness, hard work, and so on—still play an important role, but in conjunction with broad patterns of economic change, as we have argued.

Are Conservative Politics a Reexpression of Racism?

The core values we have mentioned, however, are fairly benign. By another interpretation there is a less benign core value that has driven the move to the right: racism, a value whose political effects would not appear to depend on the economic experience of the forgotten majority. By this analysis, white voters, over the last several decades, have come to see both the Democratic party and activist government as agents of minority, particularly black, interests. Since most white voters are racist, the argument posits, substantial numbers of these voters have been led to desert both the party and the activist policies it espouses.

Here, too, the story has a surface plausibility. It's hard to deny that racism remains a strong force in America today, or that appeals to race have figured prominently in the achievement of various recent political outcomes—from welfare reform, to burgeoning prison populations, to cutbacks in all manner of social programs. Nor is there any question that, in terms of timing, the advent of the civil rights revolution coincided with the initial collapse of the Democratic presidential coalition in the late 1960s. Finally, and most compelling, Democratic presidential support among blacks since the early 1960s has remained steady[29] (in fact, *increased* slightly), while Democratic presidential support among whites, as we observed earlier, has dropped precipitously (as shown in Table 2.1), by 13 percentage points.

But while all this seems at least consistent with the racial backlash story, it by no means establishes it as the dominant explanation of eroding Democratic strength. Indeed, there are a number of reasons to think otherwise. One is that this argument is broadly applicable to whites but does not explain why the political shifts were concentrated so heavily among the white working class. Another is the inconvenient fact that, by virtually every measure one might care to use, racial tolerance has increased drastically and racial prejudice has decreased drastically among all sectors of the white population in the last four decades. Seen in this light, racism seems unlikely to have been driving political change over this entire period.

Consider these examples. In 1958, 44 percent of whites said they might or would definitely move if a black person became their next-door neighbor; in 1997, the figure was 1 percent. In 1961, 50 percent of respondents said they would vote for a well-qualified black person for president; by 1987, the figure had risen to 79 percent. In 1963, 63 percent of whites said whites and blacks should attend the same schools. The corresponding figure in 1985 was 92 percent. Also in 1963, 60 percent of whites agreed that whites have a right to keep blacks out of their neighborhood; by 1988, that figure had dropped to 24 percent.[30] The list goes on and on, but all the changes tend to be large and all are in the same direction: *more* tolerance, *less* racism.[31] Moreover, where available, data indicate that the forgotten majority moved even more heavily in this direction than did other whites.

These are impressive changes. Indeed, comprehensive analyses of public opinion change[32] establish that racial attitudes are the area of public opinion where the largest and most consistently liberal attitude changes have taken place. And Brooks[33] shows that liberal changes in these attitudes have actually helped Democrats counter the effects of Republican trends over the last several decades. Thus, much past the late 1960s and early 1970s, when this liberalization of racial attitudes really began to overwhelm the backward views of part of the white population, it is difficult to see racial backlash as the key driving force in politics.

A standard reply to this observation, among those who wish to maintain the political centrality of racism, is that racism has simply changed its stripes. That is, the overt racist opinions measured by the questions just cited may indeed have declined, but they have been replaced by a "new" or "symbolic" racism that conjoins traditional American values, such as individualism, to anti-black sentiments. In this view, developed most fully by political scientists Donald Kinder and Lynn Sanders,[34] positive responses to statements like "Irish, Italian, Jewish and many other minorities overcame prejudice and worked their way up. Blacks should do the same without any special favors" or "It's really a matter of some people not trying hard enough; if blacks would only try harder they could be just as well off as whites" indicate a broad embrace of a more subtle "new racism" that drives political behavior.

The problem with this conclusion is that statements like these tap into attitudes toward government at least as much as they tap into racial attitudes. Indeed, a thorough analysis of the "new racism" argument by political scientists Paul Sniderman, Edward Carmines, William Howell, and Will Morgan[35] shows that endorsement of such statements has much less to do with white hostility toward blacks than with hostility toward a specifically liberal view of the role of government in racial matters. In short, these authors establish that the so-called new racism is mostly about political values and attitudes toward government, not racism.

Again, this is not to say that negative racial stereotypes are absent from our politics. In his book *Why Americans Hate Welfare*,[36] political scientist Martin Gilens convincingly establishes that the stereotype (on the part of whites) that blacks don't try hard enough and tend to be lazy has played a strong role in generating opposition to welfare spending. But even here the force of the stereotype seems limited to specific programs. For example, as Gilens also notes, whites have been quite willing to support spending[37] on anti-poverty programs that are closely associated with blacks but that do not tap into stereotypes about work effort, such as Head Start. Nor has the elimination of welfare done much to restore high levels of support for activist government. Pernicious and pervasive as they continue to be—although, again, the situation is improving—racial stereotypes just don't seem to have the strength or breadth to explain the much broader decline in support for Democrats and activist government.

A softer version of the racism thesis—indeed, so soft that its stance on the actual role of racism *per se* is ambiguous—is the analysis of racial "issue evolution" offered by political scientists Edward Carmines and James Stimson and popularized, to some extent, by journalists Thomas and Mary Edsall.[38] This argument holds that attitudes about race-related issues like equal employment, school integration, the role of the civil rights movement, and feelings about black militants decisively shaped the changing partisan loyalties of voters after 1964 and were essentially responsible for white flight out of the Democratic party.

Political scientist Alan Abramowitz[39] has observed sensibly that establishing (as Carmines and Stimson do) that Democratic and Republican partisans have become more polarized on race-related issues since 1964 does not mean that white voters were therefore choosing parties and casting votes on that basis. Other issues could conceivably have been as important as, if not more important than, racial issues in motivating them. Abramowitz's analysis establishes that, indeed, this was the case and that conservatism on race-related issues—at least in the 1980s—was actually comparatively unimportant in determining white voters' partisan loyalties and voting decisions. In fact, the most important issue in Abramowitz's analyses is consistently conservatism on the role of government: White voters who preferred lower taxes to more services and who favored a less active government in areas such as health insurance, jobs, and living standards moved away from the Democrats during the Reagan years.

A simple racial backlash story therefore does not work as an overarching explanation of conservative political change over a several-decade time span. However, by reconsidering the core values cited earlier, we can see how race has still played a role in that change. For most white Americans, the civil rights revolution and the enhanced social status of blacks have been consistent with their increasingly liberal values in this area. Yet some government actions and priorities related to race, such as welfare and racial preferences in employment and education, have been perceived as contradicting deeply held values concerning the importance of merit and deservedness in allocating social resources. This perception has contributed to declining support for activist government in areas directly related to race, or where there is a direct connection to racial stereotypes about black work effort. But, as research suggests, this aversion to a specific and limited set of programs does not explain the larger issue of generally weak support for activist government and for the Democratic party [40] or, further, why this weakness has been so heavily concentrated among the forgotten majority.

Are Americans More Ideologically Conservative?

Another broad argument about the turn to the right that leaves out the forgotten majority and its economic experience is the claim that core political ideologies have changed. Specifically, because of the perceived excesses and failures of the welfare state, Americans now hold philosophically more conservative views about the role of government in the economy and in society in general. There is much to recommend this argument. More people currently identify themselves and their views of government as conservative than was the case twenty-five years ago. As Chart 2.2 shows, among National Election Studies respondents willing to offer an ideological description, the number of people describing themselves as "conservative"—and therefore, presumably, having a relatively skeptical attitude toward government—rose from about 37 percent in 1972[41] to 44 percent in 1996. Moreover, the strength of the relationship between self-reported ideology and party identification has increased; that is, conservatives are more likely than they used to be to identify with the Republican party, thus accentuating the political significance of this trend.[42]

CHART 2.2   Self-Reported Ideology, 1972–96

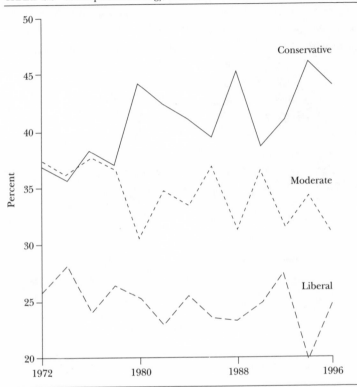

Source: Authors' analysis of National Election Studies data, 1972–96.

Other questions that directly tap into the role of government show an even more pronounced rightward move among voters. For example, since 1976, CBS/*New York Times* and other polling organizations have been asking: "Would you say you favor smaller government with fewer services, or larger government with many services?" (see Chart 2.3). In April of 1976, right before the election of Jimmy Carter, slightly more people (44 percent) favored larger government than smaller government (40 percent). But

CHART 2.3   Percentages of Those Who Favor Larger or Smaller Government, 1976–96

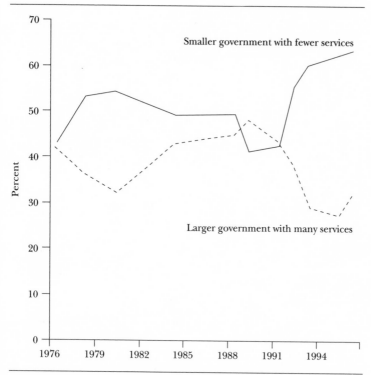

Source: Everett Carll Ladd and Karlyn Bowman, *What's Wrong? A Survey of American Satisfaction and Complaint* (Washington, D.C.: AEI Press, 1998).

two decades later, before the reelection of the only subsequent Democratic president, the proportion favoring smaller government stood at 63 percent compared to just 32 percent favoring larger government. This shift—23 percentage points in a conservative, anti-government direction over the twenty-year period—is a substantial one.

CHART 2.4   Trust in Federal Government, 1964–96

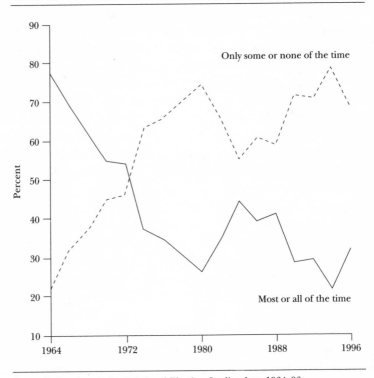

Source: Authors' analysis of National Election Studies data, 1964–96.

Then there is the famous "trust in government" question pioneered by the NES: "How much do you think you can trust the government in Washington to do what is right—just about always, most of the time, or only some of the time?" In 1964, almost eight in ten individuals (four-fifths)[43] said they trusted the government in Washington to do the right thing most or all of the time (see Chart 2.4). By 1994, that figure had plummeted to just over one-fifth before recovering to a little less than one-third in 1996. The total change over the 1964–96 period[44] was an amazing decline of over 45 percentage points in public trust in government.

Two other classic NES questions that go back to 1964—"Would you say the government is pretty much run by a few big interests looking out for themselves or that it is run for the benefit of all the people?" and "Do you think that people in government waste a lot of money we pay in taxes, waste some of it, or don't waste very much of it?"—show a similar anti-government trend, though smaller in magnitude. And there are a host of survey questions of more recent vintage that suggest the same anti-government mind-set. For example, 57 percent say they have just a little or no confidence that when the government in Washington decides to solve a problem, it will actually be solved. And 72 percent say that, in general, the federal government creates more problems than it solves. Similarly, 64 percent say that when something is run by the government, it is usually inefficient and wasteful. Finally, 58 percent think that government is doing too many things best left to individuals and business.[45]

So far, so good. These trends seem very consistent with what we are seeking to explain: the continued weakness of activist government and an activist Democratic party in the current political landscape. The problem is that the *content* of these conservative attitudes is not clear. When voters express anti-government views, are they endorsing a libertarian view of the role of government, whereby government is intrinsically a poor agent for solving problems and should therefore always play a very limited role? This really would be a shift in core ideology. Or is their verdict on government basically performance-driven and fundamentally nonideological, meaning that the role of government could (and should) vary with the scale of problems and competence of government? If so, this would reflect a shift in people's judgments of government's effectiveness, not in their core ideology about government's role.

We have four decades of survey data from Gallup, Roper, Harris, the National Opinion Research Center, the National Election Studies, ABC, NBC, CBS, and numerous other sources that allow us to evaluate these two possibilities. A massive review of these survey data by political scientist William Mayer[46] turns up much evidence that voters have come to harbor negative views of many government actions but little evidence that they have fundamentally rejected the importance of government's role.[47] Along the same lines, Brooks[48] provides a convincing and very detailed demonstration that the rise of conservative "ideology" among the electorate can be tied to changing evaluations of the respective abilities of the Democratic and Republican parties to solve important social problems. Finally, the Pew Research Center's 1998 study,[49] *Deconstructing Distrust: How Americans View Government*, the most complete examination yet of the content of current anti-government animus, provides further evidence that people are mostly displeased with government's problem-solving abilities.

In this survey, respondents' ratings of the federal government's job performance are most closely related to distrust of government and second most closely related to cynicism about public officials and their commitment to serving the public. Running far behind in the survey were more ideological items such as views about government power and taxes.

The Pew study also suggests why perception of government's effectiveness is so important to voters' feelings about government—they *expect* a lot out of government, so they are disappointed when they don't get it. For example, data in the report show that public desire for government services and activism has remained high over the last thirty years. Indeed, there are *more* people today who believe that the government should see that no one is without food, clothing, and shelter (72 percent) than there were at the height of the Great Society era, in 1964 (68 percent). Similarly, 74 percent today agree that the federal government has a responsibility to do away with poverty, compared to 73 percent in 1964.

Further data from the Pew study indicate that people continue to believe that the federal government, rather than state and local government, private industry, or individuals/community groups, should be primarily responsible for managing the economy (68 percent), ensuring access to affordable health care (58 percent), conserving the country's natural resources (52 percent), and providing a decent standard of living for the elderly (46 percent). Moreover, people consistently believe that there is a gap between how high a priority they think these policy goals should have in governmental practice and how high a priority they actually do have in governmental practice. As Table 2.3 shows, 75 percent believe ensuring access to affordable health care should have a high governmental priority, whereas just 15 percent believe that goal does have a high priority. Similarly, 72 percent believe providing the elderly with a decent standard of living should be a high priority, compared to only 17 percent who believe it does have a high priority; 76 percent believe conserving natural resources should have a high priority, compared to 24 percent who believe it does; 65 percent believe reducing poverty should be a high priority, compared to just 16 percent who believe it does; and so on. The high expectations for the federal government reported earlier, combined with these huge priority gaps, hardly suggest a libertarian public. Rather, and more straightforwardly, they suggest a public frustrated with government's ability to get the job done.

More support for this view can be gleaned from studies of public attitudes toward domestic spending. The counterintuitive point made by most of these studies is how *little* overall change has occurred in support of domestic spending, despite some ups and downs during various periods. Mayer's study of public opinion in-

TABLE 2.3   The Priority That Government Actually Gives to Policy
Goals Versus the Priority It Should Give, 1997 (in percentages)

	Actually Gives *High Priority*	*Should Give* *High Priority*	*Priority* *Gap*
Ensuring access to affordable health care	15	75	–60
Providing the elderly a decent standard of living	17	72	–55
Conserving natural resources	24	76	–52
Reducing poverty	16	65	–49
Setting academic standards for schools	20	68	–48
Reducing juvenile deliquency	13	60	–47
Ensuring safe food and medicine	50	90	–40
Ensuring everyone can afford college	11	50	–39

Source: Pew Research Center, *Deconstructing Distrust: How Americans View
Government* (Washington, D.C.: Pew Research Center for the People and
the Press, 1998).

dicates little change in support for such spending in the 1960s, followed by a moderate decline in the 1970s and a countervailing *rise*
in the 1980s.[50] The end result was that public support for domestic spending in the late 1980s seemed remarkably similar to what
it had been in the early 1970s, if not somewhat higher.

Sociologist Tom Smith's[51] review of General Social Survey
(GSS) data on public support for public spending (1973–98) revealed that the public has consistently felt that too little, rather
than too much, money is being spent in most specific program
areas.[52] (The full set of items, with 1998 data, is shown in Table
2.4.) Smith found that support for public spending peaked

TABLE 2.4   Views on Government Spending, 1998 (in percentages)

	Too Little	About Right	Too Much	Net Score[1]
Education	73	21	7	66
Health	70	24	7	63
Environment	65	28	8	57
Halting the rising crime rate	64	29	7	56
Social Security	60	33	7	53
Assistance to the poor	63	26	11	51
Dealing with drug addiction	61	30	10	51
Law enforcement	57	35	8	49
Drug rehabilitation	56	32	12	44
Solving the problems of the big cities	52	35	14	38
Highways and bridges	41	49	10	30
Parks and recreation	36	57	6	30
Mass transportation	35	55	10	25
Improving the conditions of blacks	37	45	18	29
Assistance to blacks	29	46	25	4
Assistance to big cities	22	45	33	−11
National defense	19	49	32	−13
Space exploration program	12	47	42	−30
Welfare	16	38	46	−30
Foreign aid	7	25	68	−61

[1] Net score is calculated by subtracting percentage responding too much from the percentage responding too little. Substractions were made prior to rounding.
Source: Tom W. Smith, "Trends in National Spending Priorities, 1973–1998," unpublished manuscript, National Opinion Research Center, Chicago, 1999.

around 1990, with those saying "too little spending" outnumbering those saying "too much spending" by an average of 25 percentage points for all spending areas and 40 points for domestic social spending[53] alone. This was followed by a decline in the

1990–94 period that left those saying "too little spending" still outnumbering those saying "too much spending" by an average of 17 percentage points for all spending areas and 26 points for domestic social spending in 1994—pretty close to where spending support was in the early 1970s when the GSS began collecting these data. It is worth noting that the 1994 data, which still reflect considerable support for public spending, were collected at the very height of the "Republican revolution" against the federal government! As Smith puts it: "Rather than less spending, what the public wants is spending that works."

Finally, data from the period between 1994 and 1998 show a modest increase in support for public spending. We may now be heading back toward the 1990 highs in spending support cited earlier—suggesting that the public's appetite for government spending on worthy projects has not diminished over the years, even if their confidence in the efficacy of that spending has.

This brings us back to the issue of the content of the American public's current conservatism. It seems clear from the evidence presented here that this conservatism reflects people's judgments of how well the government has worked in the recent past—and is thus what might be termed a "pragmatic conservatism"—rather than a fundamentally hostile view of the role of government. Indeed, the evidence suggests that Americans can be characterized as liberal in terms of what they want from government, conservative in their views of its ability to solve current problems, and not clearly one or the other in their view of government's basic role.

But why has this pragmatic conservatism had such special and spectacular political effects on the forgotten majority? What has happened to these voters, either alone or in combination with other factors, that led them to judge the actions of government so harshly? So far, neither demographic shifts nor value changes nor even racial backlashes seem qualified to provide the driving force for such a change. We believe the missing ingredient here is the economic experience of America's forgotten majority and how that experience has contradicted their values.

The Missing Ingredient:
Slow and Unequally Distributed Growth

In the first chapter, we introduced the Great Slowdown, Growing Apart, and the resulting Great Divide between the fortunes of college-educated workers and non-college-educated ones that has defined American economic experience since the early 1970s. These huge economic changes strike us as a missing—and crucial—basis for explaining the dramatic political shifts of the last generation. If the forgotten majority has, in fact, become stalled on the economic escalator to the middle class in the last generation, such a change would conflict with core values such as reward for hard work and lead to resentment of ineffective government and of those people whom government has (apparently) been helping instead. But first we need to determine whether and how much the forgotten majority actually suffered from these economic trends.

Economic data indicate that it has indeed suffered. Forgotten majority workers saw their real median wages drop 9 percent between 1979 and 1998, while college-educated whites saw their median wages *rise* 12 percent (see Chart 2.5). Similarly, despite increased work effort (more women in the paid labor force), the real median household income[54] of the forgotten majority grew by just 4 percent between 1979 and 1998,[55] while that of whites with a college degree increased by 22 percent (see Chart 2.6).

As the charts show, these educational contrasts continue to be stark when men and women are considered separately. For example, while women overall generally did better than men in the 1980s and 1990s, forgotten majority women's wages still went up

CHART 2.5   Real Median Wage Trends Among Whites, 1979–98

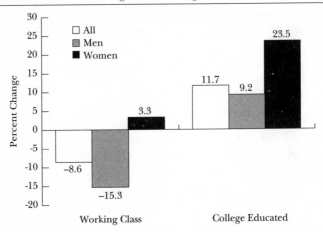

Source: Authors' analysis of CPS Outgoing Rotation Group files, 1979–98.

CHART 2.6   Real Median Household Income Trends Among Whites, 1979–98

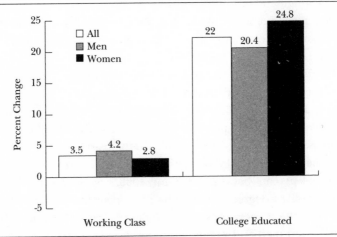

Source: Authors' analysis of CPS data, March Supplement, 1979–98.

only a very modest 3 percent over the time period and their household income went up a similarly modest amount, while their college-educated counterparts saw their wages rise an astonishing 24 percent and their household incomes, 25 percent.

The situation was exceptionally bleak for forgotten majority men. They saw their wages drop an incredible 15 percent between 1979 and 1998, while their college-educated counterparts enjoyed a gain of 9 percent. Similarly, the median household income of working-class white men inched up only 4 percent between 1979 and 1998, while that of white men with a college education shot up 20 percent. Thus, a typical white working-class man in 1979 lived in a household with an income of $44,500,[56] but after nineteen years of economic growth his 1998 counterpart was doing barely better, having an income of just $46,400. In contrast, a typical college-educated white man lived in a household with $64,000 in income in 1979, a figure that rose by over $13,000 to $77,000 by 1998.

It is not hard to imagine how these changes must have felt to the forgotten majority man. As at least part of America was becoming ever more affluent, an affluence that was well covered on television and in the evening news, he did not seem to be making much progress. What could he be doing wrong to be faring so poorly? Why couldn't he afford what others could? And why were they moving ahead while he was standing still?

Economist Frank Levy,[57] in his 1998 book *The New Dollars and Dreams*, provides additional information on the plight of forgotten majority men. He shows that, in the eighteen years from 1979 to 1997, white men in forgotten majority occupations made almost no progress or negative progress in earnings, compared to tremendous progress over the three decades prior to 1979. Technicians' average earnings rose from $20,000 to $35,000 between 1949 and 1979, but then, over the next eighteen years, increased only $2,000. And police, fire, and other protective service workers' earnings shot up from $19,000 to $32,000 in the first period; over the whole of the second, they increased by only $1,000.[58] Imagine how it must have felt to the fireman accustomed to healthy annual raises and ever-rising living standards to suddenly find himself barely keeping up with inflation.

And these were the "good" occupations. Average earnings of salesworkers increased from $19,000 to $32,000 between 1949 and 1979, and then actually *dropped* by $1,000 by 1997; those of administrative support workers went from $19,000 to $30,000, and then fell by $3,000; and those of skilled blue-collar workers, such as mechanics, machinists, and carpenters, rose from $19,000 to $32,000, and then also fell by $3,000. Nor were these declines in average earnings by occupation wholly explained by declining starting wages; they also included massive declines for older workers, with considerable and growing work experience. For example, the typical fifty-year-old white male high school graduate in 1996 was earning about $31,000—$2,000 to $3,000 *less* than he was making at forty years of age in 1986. A decade of hard work had actually reduced his living standard!

And to add to his woes, there was a 10 percent greater chance that he now lacked health insurance. This outcome reflects a general trend away from employer-provided health coverage that has compounded the woes of forgotten majority workers. Along with their lack of progress on basic measures like wages and income, they now face a world where they are at substantial risk of not having, or of losing, access to affordable health care.

Not to mention their *additional* risk of lacking pension coverage. Less than half of all private-sector American workers now have access to a pension plan through their employer, and the situation is even worse for the forgotten majority.[59] Moreover, those who are covered by a pension are increasingly likely to have to fund that pension themselves, through a "defined contribution" 401(k)-type plan, rather than to receive a guaranteed pension on their retirement ("defined benefit"), as was over-whelmingly the case twenty-five years ago.

These data on economic progress (or lack thereof) among whites match up well with the political changes we have been in-vestigating. Among those whites for whom the post-1973 eco-nomic world has generally been hard, the Democratic party has lost its appeal, while among those for whom it's been something close to a disaster—white *men*—a complete meltdown in Demo-cratic support levels has occurred. There's very little mystery here, but no small amount of rationality. These voters really *had* become stalled on the economic escalator to the middle class, and "activist" Democrats weren't doing anything about it. And with the forgotten majority workers' own incomes stagnant or de-clining, they became very reluctant to pay for programs that they didn't think worked, or worked for everyone but them.

But Doesn't the Late 1990s Change All That?

The last years of the 1990s, however, have been famously good ones, both for the U.S. economy as a whole and for the typical worker and family. Unemployment has dipped to levels lower than any seen in the post-1973 era, and inflation has easily been held in check. And this has happened while the economy has ex-panded rapidly, at over a 4 percent annual rate, and productivity has grown at about a 2.6 percent annual rate. The combination of rapid growth and tight labor markets has been exceptionally good for workers, particularly from 1997 onward, with real wages rising at about a 2 percent (or more) annual rate.[60] Does such a turnaround reverse the economic dynamic just described?

If sustained indefinitely, indeed it would. However, several good years are not sufficient, by themselves, to bring about such a reversal. First, consider the fact that, despite the euphoric rhetoric about unprecedented levels of economic performance ("These *are* the good old days," commented a writer in *Fortune* magazine), the U.S. economy in the 1990s, considered over the course of the entire business cycle, has, in fact, performed only somewhat better than the recent past and downright poorly compared to the pre-1973 U.S. economy.

Take economic growth. As we showed in Chart 1.1, the average economic growth rate over the entire 1990s business cycle was no higher than in the 1980s and the 1970s and much lower than in the 1960s and 1950s. A comparison of productivity growth rates also shows that productivity growth in the 1990s, while an improvement over the anemic 1980s and 1970s, has remained substantially below that of the pre-1973 period.

So, on the basis of these measures of economic growth, there is no compelling reason to say that the 1990s mark a qualitative break from the rest of the post-1973 era. Of course, it is *possible* that the last several years *do* mark entrance into a new, fast-growth economic world. But these measures suggest that it is way too early to make such a judgment—or for the average person to act with the confidence that would follow from having entered such a world.

Nor do measures of individual well-being—notably, wages and incomes—suggest that the 1990s, considered as a whole, mark a qualitative break from the 1980s and 1970s. This is particularly so for the forgotten majority. Consider wages. While it is true that 1997 and 1998 were excellent years for wage growth among all workers, the median hourly wage for the new white working class at the end of 1998 was still 2 percent *below* its level in 1989, the peak of the last business cycle. And the situation was even worse for new white working-class men: Their median wage was still 6 percent below its 1989 level. In short, despite all the positive economic progress in 1997 and 1998, the typical forgotten majority male at that point had about $1,700 less in buying power than he did nine years before (figured on a full-time, full-year basis).

Income data are similarly uninspiring. The latest data available for the forgotten majority, through 1998, show that while median household income for the group rose in each of the preceding five years, it was still only slightly above its 1989 level. Some point to these five consecutive years of income growth as indicative of a truly new and better economy. Comparisons to the 1980s, however, make this claim problematic. Overall median household income rose 10 percent between 1993 and 1998, only slightly more than the 9 percent between 1983 and 1988. Such comparisons cast doubt on the assertion that we have unequivocally entered a new economic era.

And wages and income hardly tap into the totality of economic challenges still faced by the forgotten majority. Insecurity about health-care coverage continues to grow to the point where, according to the latest figures,[61] an incredible 44 million Americans, over 16 percent of the population, now lack health insurance. Similarly, the majority of forgotten majority private-sector workers continue to lack pension coverage, and those that do have it are increasingly likely to lack a guaranteed income in their retirement. The rapid shift toward "defined contribution" plans, where the employer simply makes contributions to an employee's retirement savings, rather than guaranteeing a yearly pension upon retirement ("defined benefit"), is taking care of that.

Finally, the news concerning inequality is particularly damning for the thesis that the 1990s represent a complete break from post-1973 economic trends. Income inequality, for example, was essentially unchanged in the last year (1998) for which such data are available—as it has been ever since the current spurt of income growth began (1993)—and it remains substantially higher than it was in 1989.[62] At this point, about half of all money income goes to the top 20 percent of households and more than one-fifth goes to just the top 5 percent. In contrast, only about one-eighth of income goes to the entire bottom 40 percent. The distribution of wealth, as opposed to money income, is even more skewed: Almost two-fifths (39 percent) of wealth is held by the top 1 percent of Americans.

Wage inequality has also continued to be a problem. Although those on the bottom of the wage distribution have been making good progress, the top has continued to grow away from the middle.[63] Indeed, the top-middle ratio is now substantially higher than it was in 1989 and is close to its post-1973 high.[64]

Any claims that recent economic performance marks a permanent change are therefore premature. While the fast and relatively equally shared economic growth of the last several years allows us to glimpse what a *good* new economy might look like, with broadly shared prosperity accompanying rapid technological change, it is too early to say it is here. Considered over the course of the 1990s, the missing ingredient—an economy of relatively slow growth, stagnating living standards, and rising inequality—is alive and well and still relevant to the economic experience of the forgotten majority.

This is why so many of these voters continue to worry: about earning enough money to lead the kind of life they want, about the impact of globalization, about not having enough money for retirement, about being unable to save enough money to put a child through college, about being unable to afford necessary health care when a family member gets sick.[65] Their economic situation, while improved, has not been fundamentally altered.

That said, it should be stressed that the last several good years have had a genuinely positive effect on the outlook of forgotten majority workers. Finally, the economy seems to be working in a way that is consistent with their values; their labor is being rewarded in a way that just hasn't been seen in a generation or so (even when incomes were rapidly increasing for several years during the Reagan era, wages were actually declining). This has promoted a softening in attitudes toward government as well as an interest in new government initiatives that, as we shall see, is at war with the forgotten majority's continued suspicion of government's effectiveness.

Completing the Story

Armed with this missing ingredient, we are now ready to complete the story behind the increasing lack of support for activist government and the party identified with activist government, the Democratic party. This story not only includes a role for all the other factors we have discussed that make up the current conventional wisdom but also, by bringing in the forgotten majority and its economic travails, considerably enriches that conventional analysis. Certainly, values are important, not so much because they have changed but because they help explain why the forgotten majority has reacted as it has to its post-1973 economic difficulties. Certainly race plays a role, not so much because of unchanging, albeit more covert, racism but because of the forgotten majority's rejection of a race-based liberalism that appeared to contradict its values and hold out little promise of improving its situation. Increasing conservatism, too, plays a role, not as an ideological rejection of government but as a pragmatically conservative distaste for government's effectiveness in solving problems, particularly those of the forgotten majority. Finally, the suburbs play a key role, not because the shift to the suburbs increases the influence of intrinsically more conservative voters but because that's where forgotten majority voters now live.

The story starts with the first shock to the Democratic coalition in the late 1960s. The rapid social change and social conflicts of that period, not least those around race, did indeed lead to a sharp decline in forgotten majority support for the Democrats in the 1968 and 1972 elections—but they had much less effect on support for activist government. Recall the domestic activism of

Richard Nixon—very impressive by today's standards—or his pronouncement that "we're all Keynesians now."

Even with this setback, the Democrats could potentially have recovered and renewed their commitment to activist government, though perhaps not on the scale of the Great Society and McGovern's 1972 campaign program. Recall that social values and racial attitudes were continuing their great liberalization, thereby providing a long-term basis for reconciling Democrats—given some moderation in the party's program—with the forgotten majority on "social" issues. But the ground was shifting under the Democrats' feet. Even as they struggled back to power under Jimmy Carter, taking advantage of the Watergate scandals and the Republicans' close proximity to the recession of 1973, the economy was changing fundamentally in the ways we have described in this chapter. The result was a second severe shock to the Democratic coalition.

Why did these new economic trends transmit a shock, not only to the Democrats but, even more so, to the whole support base for activist government? Because government did almost nothing to relieve them. It seemed, by turns, monumentally indifferent, hopelessly feeble, and even insulting to that majority's core values—fair reward for effort, the centrality of hard work and individual achievement, social responsibility and order, equal opportunity for all.

By the end of the 1970s, forgotten majority voters had truly entered an economic world radically different from the one enjoyed by the preceding (or any previous) generation. Slow growth, declining wages, stagnating living standards, and, at the time, high and variable inflation and high home mortgage interest rates (housing, again, being the only real form of "wealth" that most U.S. workers possess) were battering them economically. The great postwar escalator to the middle class had basically stopped. And the response of "activist" government continued to be tepid.

Or, worse, instead of honoring and encouraging core values in these changing times, it focused on liberal social programs to help gays, women, and minorities.[66] The latter view was easy to cultivate among forgotten majority voters in the late 1970s, since many of them had already become convinced, even prior to 1973, that the Democrats were out of touch with mainstream values, due to their perceived association with extremist elements of the civil rights and antiwar movements.[67] Hence the forgotten majority's pragmatically conservative judgment on government, even as most of these voters were actually moving to adopt much more liberal social values, as we saw earlier.

But why didn't this pragmatic conservatism affect blacks, given that they, too, were affected by these economic changes? The reason is that the civil rights struggle and the War on Poverty had forged special ties between blacks and the Democrats' brand of activist government.

This explains the rock-steady support of blacks for the Democratic party indicated in Table 2.1. The government and the Democratic party were then—and are today—viewed as integral to advancing black economic and social interests, no matter how unspectacular the record of overall progress, and shielding them from the more reactionary forces gathered in the GOP. Black workers, no less than white ones, would like to get something more out of the economy. But their particular and natural concern for maintaining their civil rights, and for remediating racism, makes them much "softer" on the Democrats' failed performance.

By contrast, whites—who lacked a series of recent experiences that would have led them to see government and the Democrats as their special benefactors—judged that performance harshly. This was especially true for those—our forgotten majority—who fared the worst in the post-1973 period and therefore had the most to blame the Democrats for. Indeed, among these voters, whose attachments to the Democratic party dated from the universalistic economic programs of the New Deal, a sense evolved that Democrats were no longer about such programs and were not really "their" party anymore.

This dynamic only intensified in the 1980s as Ronald Reagan swept into office, administered his historic tax cuts, and launched a frontal attack on the funding and legitimacy of the welfare state. This policy shift was accompanied, over the course of the 1980s, by a continued worsening of the forgotten majority's economic situation and a rapid rise in inequality. As it turned out, these developments simply added fuel to the fire of pragmatic conservatism, as forgotten majority voters became increasingly convinced that government simply had no answers to their problems. All they could reasonably hope for, they concluded, was to play catch-up when economic times were relatively good—as they were after the 1981–82 recession—and just try to get by over the long haul. The major parties' response to the changed economy successfully lowered hopes for government almost as quickly as it disappointed them.

The resulting pragmatic conservatism of the forgotten majority was further fanned by racially charged issues like crime and welfare (recall the infamous Willie Horton ad during the 1988 presidential campaign), which underscored to these voters that the Democratic approach to government was inconsistent with their values—not with their values about equality (which by this point had become relatively liberal) but with their values about reward for effort and punishment for wrongdoing.

The Democrats struggled desperately throughout the 1980s to stem this tide. They both defended the welfare state and attempted to escape blame for its shortcomings. The balancing act was not successful. It was only the recession of 1990–91, and the associated economic pessimism, that allowed Bill Clinton to win the presidency in 1992. In so doing, he and his fellow Democrats heavily emphasized the negative economic trends of the 1980s (rising inequality, declining wages, stagnant incomes) and promised to reverse them with a new economic model stressing public investment, worker training, universal health-care coverage, and regulation of global integration to safeguard American living standards. That, in conjunction with a cleverly refurbished image that put to rest much of the values conflict around social issues, was enough to vanquish the Republicans.

Since then, the Democrats have made excellent progress in defusing white workers' lingering suspicions of their values around issues like crime and welfare, as crime rates have dropped and the welfare program has been completely eliminated. But they have been less successful in constructing an economic model consistent with the values of the forgotten majority. The result, as we shall see, is that the Democrats and activist government still lack a strong base among these voters and find themselves in a cul-de-sac where both policy actions and political prospects are limited. Of course, the Republicans have not constructed such an economic model either, and they now lack the overwhelming values advantage they once had with the forgotten majority. The upshot is the stalemate that characterizes American politics today. We describe the development of this stalemate in the next two chapters, where the elections of the 1990s are described and dissected.

THREE

Did the Forgotten Majority Matter in the 1990s? Part 1: The Elections of 1992 and 1994

[O]ur middle class seems to be better off. . . . The economy is the smoke and mirrors issue. . . . Clinton and the Democrats won in 1992 by claiming a new political moderation. . . . [He] was not moderate on the values issues . . . because the Clinton administration dropped the ball on the values issues, the Democrats were decimated in 1994.

—BEN WATTENBERG, AUTHOR OF *Values Matter Most*, 1995[1]

WE HAVE ARGUED THAT THE GREAT DIVIDE between those with and without a four-year college degree has created a new white working class that forms the majority of voters. We have further established that considering the economic experience and values of the forgotten majority considerably enriches the conventional story about anti-government political change in the last several decades.

But what of the 1990s? It is possible that the forgotten majority drove politics in the 1980s but has been relatively inactive in the 1990s, with other voter groups becoming the volatile or swing elements in politics. In this chapter and the next, we investigate this possibility by looking at the role of the forgotten majority in each election of the 1990s, relying especially on detailed analyses of exit poll and Census Bureau data.

First, we turn to the elections of 1992 and 1994, two elections that witnessed remarkable volatility among the U.S. electorate. In 1992, the Republican presidential coalition, dominant throughout the 1980s, shattered, with George Bush suffering the third-largest decline in support (16 percentage points) for an incumbent president in U.S. electoral history. Then, in 1994, the Democratic congressional coalition, dominant for over four decades, broke up, producing a fifty-two-seat loss—its largest since 1946—and Republican control of Congress for the first time in forty-two years. We will show that forgotten majority voters were far and away the most volatile segment of the electorate in this time period—the real "swing voters" during these momentous political events.

We begin with an analysis of the 1992 election, the first Democratic presidential victory since 1976. This is in part a story of the rise of the "New Democrats" and how their success framed the Democratic approach to the 1992 election and beyond.

The Rise of the New Democrats

Recall the political events that shook the Democratic party from the late 1960s to the mid-1980s: the Nixon victories of 1968 and 1972; the tax revolt of the late 1970s; and, most traumatically for the Democrats, the Reagan victories of 1980 and 1984. These events led some in the Democratic party to conclude, by the end of this period, that there was a pressing need to realign the party and make it more appealing to voters—otherwise, the party would continue to lose, and lose badly, in national elections.

The party's solution was essentially a *marketing* response. That is, it became generally accepted that the image of the Democratic party had become a negative one in too many voters' eyes and that, therefore, the image had to be replaced with a better one. For example, instead of emphasizing social liberalism and the unqualified "rights" of various groups, the party should emphasize family and rights *with* responsibilities; instead of welfare, the party should emphasize welfare reform; instead of income distribution, economic growth; and so on. The relationship between the old, "bad" image and the proposed new image is summarized in Table 3.1.

Within the party, this marketing strategy was identified most strongly with a group called the Democratic Leadership Council (DLC), formed in 1985 by a group of politicians, including Charles Robb, Richard Gephardt, Bruce Babbitt, and Sam Nunn, and political operatives, including such key figures as Al From and Will Marshall. Once formed, the DLC quickly became a pole of attraction for the considerable number of politicians—mostly moderate to conservative and many from the South—who felt the party's image needed a drastic revamping.[2]

The drive to transform the Democratic party received considerable impetus from Michael Dukakis's poor showing in 1988. He became the poster boy within the party for traditional liberalism, for the image that had turned off a large segment of voters. This assessment of Dukakis's failings increased the level of sympathy for the DLC and other forces pushing the necessity of a new image, even among those who found the DLC's specific policy ideas wrong or incoherent or both.

Indeed, the DLC specifically framed its approach in terms of "inoculating" the Democrats from attacks in social and cultural areas, so that the party's "progressive economic message" could

TABLE 3.1   Old and New Images of the Democratic Party

Old Image	New Image
Social liberalism, for "rights"	For family, rights with responsibilities
For welfare	Welfare reform
Income redistribution	Economic growth
Big government, much spending	Lean government, "reinvent" programs
Giveaways to poor and minorities	"New covenant," hand up to willing poor
Soft on crime	Tough on crime
For special interests	Against special interests
Unpatriotic	Patriotic
Against white working/middle class	For white working/middle class

get across to voters. As William Galston and Elaine Kamarck, leading DLC intellectuals, put it:

> [A]ll too often the American people do not respond to a progressive economic message, even when Democrats try to offer it, because the party's presidential candidates fail to win their confidence in other areas such as defense, foreign policy and social values. Credibility on these issues is the ticket that will get Democratic candidates in the door to make their affirmative economic case.

Once they were in the door, that progressive economic message about promoting economic security, providing universal health coverage, increasing public investment, and fighting inequality could get across to voters, particularly the white working-class/middle-class voters who had deserted the party in large numbers.[3] Thus, in this early incarnation, the New Democrats' approach was visualized fairly specifically as an approach to appeal to the forgotten majority. As we shall see, this early focus changed considerably over the course of the 1990s, to the point where it became, ironically, almost its own mirror image, with the DLC advocating a conservative economic message to reach socially liberal, upper-middle-class suburbanites.

At the time, this emphasis on a progressive economic message made it easier for most in the party to accept some version of the DLC approach, since everyone in the party was anxious to reach the voters whom Democrats had lost in the 1970s and 1980s. If the DLC approach was the only way to get voters to listen to progressive economics, many were willing to make that compromise.

However, the more the DLC defined what *it* meant by progressive economics, the more it seemed to depart not just from the letter, but also the spirit, of post–New Deal, Democratic-style economics. In the 1989–92 period, the DLC advanced proposals to expand the earned income tax credit (EITC), but explicitly balanced that by opposing any raise in the minimum wage. The DLC also suggested some increased spending on worker training, but insisted that this had to occur through the provision of vouchers to individual workers rather than through increased spending on federal programs. It strongly supported trade expansion and the North American Free Trade Agreement (NAFTA), but was opposed to strengthening U.S. sanctions against unfair trading and labor practices. And it strongly attacked the role of unions, both private and public, as barriers to the practice of efficient economics and government. In fact, the economic views of the DLC, as they started to evolve, were increasingly coming to resemble a moderate, business-oriented Republicanism. But for a party still smarting from poor showings in three successive presidential elections, these views were relatively easy for most to overlook at the time.

To accelerate the transformation of the party's image, the DLC and allied forces adopted a confrontational internal stance against those forces most adamantly opposed to their ideas. As a result of this stance, they succeeded (and that was how they viewed it) in getting both the AFL-CIO and Jesse Jackson's Rainbow Coalition to picket the 1991 DLC convention in Cleveland.[4] Then, during the 1992 Democratic primary campaign, Bill Clinton—who had only recently stepped down from the chairmanship of the DLC—issued his famous denunciation of Sister Souljah, a now-obscure rap singer, at a public event in Washington, D.C., sponsored by Jesse Jackson.

Indeed, by the time of Clinton's acceptance speech at the 1992 Democratic convention, it is fair to say that those elements in the party most hostile to the image makeover had been thoroughly marginalized. Because of this, the party was able to unite around the themes summarized on the right-hand side of Table 3.1 (including rights with responsibilities, welfare reform, reinventing government, and being tough on crime) and elaborated at great length by Clinton in his speech. Combined with considerable economic anxieties extant at the time, these new themes provided a strong base for synthesizing a new and more appealing Democratic message for the electorate in general and the forgotten majority in particular.

Indeed, as journalist John Judis has argued,[5] this new Democratic message really had three parts: a "New Democrat" part, based on many of the DLC's ideas; an "economic populist" part (summarized in the famous pamphlet "Putting People First"), based on government activism and investment to promote economic fairness and rising living standards; and a forward-looking "economic nationalist" part, based on international activism to both promote global integration and regulate aspects of it, such as capital mobility, that posed serious threats to American living standards.[6]

This "new synthesis" was quite in tune with the inclinations of the forgotten majority and sufficiently plausible for Clinton to present himself as a viable—or, at any rate, not disastrous—alternative to an extremely unpopular incumbent.[7] The result: Enough voters deserted Bush, including a 22 percentage point drop among the forgotten majority, to hand the election to Clinton on November 3, 1992.

Perot Voters and the 1992 Election

But while the drop-off in Republican support was of historic proportions, Democrats were not the direct beneficiary. Clinton received only 43 percent of the popular vote, actually down slightly from the 45 percent that Dukakis had received in 1988.[8] In fact, in most respects, the "new" Democratic voters of 1992 looked an awful lot like the old Democratic voters of 1988.

Clinton actually did worse than Dukakis among key demographic groups. For example, among those with only a high school degree and among those with some college—the heart of the working class—Dukakis received 50 and 43 percent of the vote, respectively, compared to 43 and 41 percent for Clinton. And, breaking high school graduates down by sex, we find that Dukakis received 50 percent among both men and women, compared to 43 percent among both groups for Clinton.

Looking specifically at whites—where the collapse of Democratic support has been concentrated, of course—we see that Clinton actually did 1 point worse than Dukakis, 39 versus 40 percent. And, while Clinton did 1 point better among white men (37 versus 36 percent), he did 4 points *worse* among white women (44 versus 40 percent).

Then, looking directly at the forgotten majority, we find that Clinton's support in the key middle education groups—the overwhelming majority of the new white working class—was anemic. He received 40 percent support among white male high school graduates, compared to just 35 percent among white males with some college (the corresponding figures for women were 39 and 37 percent). And in all but one of these cases, Clinton's support was actually less than Dukakis's in 1988.

This pattern is underscored by looking at income groups:[9] Among the three middle-income groups, $15,000–$30,000, $30,000–$50,000, and $50,000–$75,000, Clinton received, respectively, 44, 40, and 40 percent. Among whites, the figures were even lower: 40, 37, and 37 percent.

In short, Clinton failed to reach the very same forgotten majority voters among whom the Democrats had been weak for years. The swing elements of these groups had been voting solidly Republican for president; in 1992, they deserted the Republicans, but huge numbers chose to vote for Ross Perot, who claimed 19 percent of the vote, the most for a third-party or independent candidate since 1912. Those who made that choice provide a privileged point of entry to understanding electoral dynamics at the time. Who were these people who deserted the Republicans but failed to attach themselves to the Democrats? What were their demographics, material circumstance, attitudes, and beliefs?

First and foremost, two-thirds of Perot's supporters were drawn from the ranks of the forgotten majority. They came from the new white working class, had low to moderate incomes, and, compared to the celebrated Reagan Democrats of the 1980s, tended to be somewhat younger and less concentrated in the Rust Belt and South. As journalist John Judis has pointed out, they were the next generation of Reagan Democrats.[10] And without these forgotten majority voters, there would have been no Perot phenomenon.

A second characteristic of Perot voters was their rapidly deteriorating economic position. Analysis of several different data sources[11] reveals that, while both Clinton and Perot voters came from groups that experienced wage losses in the 1980s and early 1990s, Perot voters' losses were uniformly larger.[12] This was partly because Perot voters were so heavily drawn from the ranks of the forgotten majority and because forgotten majority Perot voters actually did worse economically than their counterparts who voted for Bush or Clinton. For example, forgotten majority Perot voters[13] lost 10 percent in real wages between 1979 and 1992, including over 2 percent in wage losses that took place in the year immediately prior to the 1992 election. In both periods, these are larger than the wage losses sustained by similar Clinton or Bush voters.

A third characteristic of Perot voters—hardly surprising in light of the economic trends just cited—was their gloomy outlook on the economy and its future path. In the 1992 exit poll, some 70 percent of Perot voters said they thought the economy was in long-term decline rather than a temporary downturn (at the time, this pessimism was shared by Clinton voters). And in terms of prospects for the future generation, Perot voters were easily the gloomiest. Some 50 percent said they thought life for the next generation would be worse, compared to 40 percent for Clinton voters and 28 percent for Bush voters. This pattern was confirmed by later polls. A *Los Angeles Times* poll conducted in June 1993 showed 67 percent of Perot supporters expecting the next generation of Americans to have a worse standard of living than today's, compared to 55 percent of Republican supporters and 39 percent of Clinton supporters.

A fourth characteristic of Perot voters was their economic nationalism. The 1992 exit poll showed that Perot voters, by a 55 to 40 percent margin, believed that trade lost more jobs than it gained—a view they shared with Clinton voters. Later polling, especially around the NAFTA agreement, confirmed this economic nationalism; indeed, the polling suggested that it had strengthened, since Perot voters/supporters were easily the most adamant opposition to the free trade agreement.[14]

The final key characteristic of the Perot voters was the one most widely cited in the press and political discussion: their relative conservatism both on values issues and the role of government. But a close reading of their responses to exit poll and other surveys suggests that Perot voters were hardly conservative ideologues regarding either the sanctity of traditional values or the wonders of the market once freed from government constraints. Instead, their "conservatism" was largely driven by a sense that middle-class values were no longer being rewarded and that, in a very practical sense, the government was not doing its job and was therefore a waste of tax money (as opposed to not having a job to do, as free-market idealogues would contend). In other words, the typical Perot voter was precisely the kind of pragmatic conservative whose contours were sketched in the last chapter.

Thus, while Perot voters tended to agree with Bush voters on the desirability of a government that provides fewer services but taxes less (72 and 79 percent support, respectively), and while they were most likely to cite the budget deficit as a voting issue, their views on the utility of government activism tended to be midway between those of Bush and Clinton voters.[15] Asked if government neglect of domestic problems (as opposed to a values breakdown) could be held responsible for social problems in the country, for example, 50 percent of Perot voters blamed government neglect, compared to 25 percent of Bush voters and 70 percent of Clinton voters. Similarly, 50 percent of Perot voters agreed that government should do more to solve national problems, a view held by 36 percent of Bush voters and 73 percent of Clinton voters.

On hot-button social issues,[16] Perot voters looked very much like Clinton supporters. For example, Perot voters' support for abortion rights was comparable to that of Clinton voters. In addition, a majority of both Perot and Clinton voters endorsed a "hands-off" stance for government in promoting values. This finding suggests a libertarian bent to Perot voters' views on cultural values: They were skeptical of government intervention not only in the economy and society but in private lives as well.

Yet on issues related to core American values—particularly the sense that those who cleave to those values and work hard are not being rewarded properly—Perot voters and Bush voters were of the same mind. For example, in a 1993 poll,[17] 76 percent of Perot voters and 75 percent of Bush voters (compared to 59 percent of Clinton voters) agreed that "it's the middle class, not the poor, who really get a raw deal today." Sixty-nine percent of Perot voters and 70 percent of Bush voters also endorsed the view that "too many of the poor are trying to get something for nothing" (compared to 53 percent of Clinton voters).

Taken together, these demographic, economic, and attitudinal data help explain the worldview and behavior of Perot voters. These primarily forgotten majority voters were experiencing— and recognized themselves to be experiencing—a sustained stagnation, if not erosion, of their living standards. This erosion had come despite their hard work and substantial tax contributions, leading to the view that the first was unrewarded ("middle-class values in decline") and the second was a waste of money. Clearly, this "conservative" view on the part of forgotten majority voters was driven less by their ideological commitment than by a need to make sense of their life experience in America over the previous fifteen to twenty years.

And from this, their electoral behavior directly followed. Fed up with Bush and the Republicans because their administration, at the end of the day, had only seemed to worsen their problems, but unable to embrace the Democrats because that party was implicated in promoting both values and government that didn't seem to benefit them, they struck out on their own and embraced what seemed a radical alternative.

The 1994 Election: The Breakup of the New Synthesis

The administration fought for a budget that, for all its redistributive impact, cut Medicare and taxed gasoline and Social Security income and that Republicans successfully labelled "the biggest tax increase in history." The administration fought for NAFTA, which likely increased economic anxieties among blue-collar workers; it fought for the rights of gays to serve in the military and to restrict the purchase of handguns; and, finally, it fought valiantly for a health care proposal that would have assured universal health coverage but that very quickly produced a conservative reaction against government.

—STANLEY GREENBERG,
PRESIDENT CLINTON'S POLLSTER, 1992–94[18]

What led from the Democrats' 1992 election victory to their catastrophe in 1994? The basic story is one of the breakup of Clinton's carefully crafted new synthesis under political pressure from Republicans and business interests and the strain of unfavorable economic trends. The result was the massive defection of the forgotten majority from the Democratic congressional coalition.

Legislative and Policy Battles

First, the more familiar part of the story. As mentioned earlier, a key part of the Clinton campaign and the new synthesis it offered was the economic populist program known as Putting People First, summarized in a pamphlet by the same name. The administration had promised a reversal of economic misfortune for average Americans, including, of course, the forgotten majority, led by an ambitious program of domestic investment as well as by a middle-class tax cut. But the program was abandoned under pressure from Wall Street and the Federal Reserve. This prompted James Carville's famous comment that he would "like to come back in the next life as the bond market"—and there was little economic populism in 1992–94. And with little of a positive nature to focus on economically, the divisive cultural issues that Clinton had deliberately pushed off the agenda in his campaign were likely to enter as an exploitable distraction. The latter happened almost immediately—by which we mean the brouhaha over the appointments process and "gays in the military." This outcome did considerable damage to the mainstream values/New Democrat part of Clinton's new synthesis, just as the populist component began to unravel.

The initial locus for this unraveling, of course, was the titanic struggle around the 1993 budget—a struggle that blurred the image of Clinton as an economic populist to near extinction. He backed off from a tax cut and instead passed general tax as well as gas tax increases. And, even though the former applied only to the upper 2 percent of households, its lack of explicit connection to the Putting People First agenda facilitated its portrayal as another "middle-class" tax soak. Instead, virtually the entire administration justification for the budget, and its associated taxes and spending cuts, was to cut the deficit—a policy priority that essentially made the initiatives of Putting People First impossible. (The last Bush budget increased public investment by 10 percent; the 1993 Clinton budget cut it by 2 percent.)[19] And rhetorically, the ceaselessly pro-business justification for cutting the deficit—that it would calm the bond markets, keep interest rates low, increase private savings, and thereby promote business investment and expansion—suggested an intrinsically "trickle down" economic approach that undercut the basic rationale of Putting People First. As it undercut that rationale, it unwittingly turned up the volume on the forgotten majority's pragmatic conservatism—the very thing the Democrats wanted and needed to overcome.

Turning to the third component of the new synthesis, a forward-looking economic nationalism, we find that this, too, disintegrated in the bitter political battle around NAFTA. NAFTA was never popular with the public, particularly the working class, who remained opposed to it until the bitter end (43–34 percent against on the eve of the decisive House vote).[20] It passed only because of a powerful mobilization of elite opinion (from leading politicians of both parties, a majority of newspaper op-ed pages, prominent economists, and business leaders) and some outright "vote-buying" in the House. More to the point, Clinton's full-bore pressing of the issue essentially erased his economic nationalist credentials among the public. While NAFTA itself never became a voting issue, Clinton's behavior sent a negative signal to working-class Americans, including the forgotten majority, about administration interest in protecting their jobs and wages under the pressure of global integration.

Finally, the knockout blow to the administration's populist credentials came from the failed health-care reform effort. A series of tactical blunders culminated in an extremely complicated plan that the public simply did not understand or see clear benefits from. This confusion played into the hands of the Republican opposition and their allies in the health insurance industry who were able successfully to portray the reform plan as yet another big government program that would do little for ordinary working Americans.[21]

This analysis should not be taken to mean that the Clinton administration blew a lot of easy opportunities. On the contrary, the economic and political pressures it faced were very real. Moreover, as Clinton received only 43 percent of the popular vote, he started with a thin political base in a country where, as we have argued, pragmatic conservatism was still very much alive, especially among the forgotten majority. In such a climate, large compromises were inevitable and big-ticket programs like health-care reform were going to be difficult to sell. The real question was whether any of these political struggles were going to be pursued in a way that would help diminish the popular base for pragmatic conservatism. Regardless of one's views about the desirability or inevitability of what the Clinton administration actually did in the 1992–94 period,[22] the answer to this question is clearly "no." Instead of diminishing the popular base for pragmatic conservatism, the administration's actions inflamed it.

Economic Trends

The story line sketched above is a familiar one and by itself goes some way toward explaining the breakdown of Clinton's new synthesis and the Democrats' election defeat in 1994. But there is a less familiar part of the story that has to do with poor economic performance and the effects of this on the forgotten majority. In short, these economic effects further reinforced the forgotten majority's pragmatic conservatism and led to its massive rejection of the Democrats in the 1994 election.

We have stressed the importance of long-term wage decline and stagnating living standards, particularly for working-class voters on the other side of the Great Divide. But given the relatively strong economic growth and low unemployment of the 1992–94 period—an economic performance repeatedly highlighted by Clinton administration officials—hopes were high that this long-term trend would be reversed. It was not to be. The miserable experience of wage decline and income stagnation continued through the first two years of the Clinton administration. For example, between 1992 and 1994, the wage of the typical (median) worker declined an additional 3 percent. The income of the typical household also declined slightly over the same period.[23] And the Great Divide continued to grow, leaving forgotten majority workers on the short end of the stick. Their wages, for example, declined by 2 percent between 1992 and 1994, while wages for college-educated whites actually increased 1 percent.

Comparing wage and income data in 1994 with those in 1989—the peak of the previous business cycle—puts the numbers in some relief. Over this period the wage of forgotten majority workers dropped by 4 percent; and that of forgotten majority men, by a stunning 10 percent. Not surprisingly, household income for the forgotten majority was also substantially down over the time period: a sizable cut of 7 percent. Thus, despite the economic recovery touted by the Clinton administration, and the increasing involvement of the new white working class in the new economy, the situation of the forgotten majority had failed to improve significantly in the administration's first two years; indeed, in some ways it had gotten worse. Coming on top of the particularly severe income and wage losses of the 1990–91 recession, not to mention the overall stagnation in living standards since 1979, this was a bitter pill for forgotten majority workers to swallow—especially since they harbored considerable suspicion of the Democrats to begin with.

Who Deserted the Democrats?

As the 1994 election approached, then, the administration's new synthesis was in tatters. The populist strategy of Putting People First had been transmuted into a very conventional strategy of promoting business confidence and hoping the continuing economic expansion would eventually lift all the boats; the forward-looking economic nationalism of the 1992 campaign had been transmuted into a free-trade-at-all-costs commitment to NAFTA; and the New Democrat profile that Clinton had so strenuously sought to cultivate had been compromised by perceived social liberalism and a seemingly bureaucratic approach to solving social problems.

This scenario, combined with declining wages and stagnating incomes in the midst of economic growth, produced a Democratic party extraordinarily vulnerable to a Republican counterattack based on populist anti-government themes—the very themes likely to resonate with the forgotten majority. The Republicans argued, in essence, that the Democrats were more interested in promoting big government than in solving the

CHART 3.1   Change in Democratic Support by Education Group, 1992–94

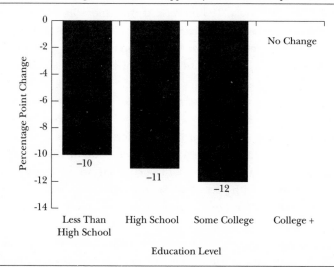

Source: Authors' analysis of 1992 VRS exit poll and 1994 VNS exit poll.

public's problems, and pointed as "evidence" to the fact that very little good had come from the first years of Clinton's term. The forgotten majority—still suffering stagnating, if not declining, living standards—was vulnerable to this argument. If government couldn't do any better than it had, why not at least reduce its size and quit wasting tax money? And if Republicans could not be looked to for any real solution to large-scale economic and social problems, could they not at least be counted on to cut taxes?

Voting patterns in the 1994 election confirm this essentially negative populist rejection of the Democrats. Working-class voters, almost all forgotten majority voters, deserted the Democrats in droves. As shown in Chart 3.1, from 1992 to 1994 Democratic support declined 10 percentage points among high school dropouts, 11 points among high school graduates, and 12 points among those with some college.

In contrast, Democratic support among college-educated individuals[24] held steady at 1992 levels. At the time, some observers suggested this as a possible basis for Democratic revival. Unfortunately for the Democrats, however, people with a four-year college degree are a relatively small part of the active electorate. While exit polls routinely show them as the single largest education group—43 percent, for example, in a 1994 exit poll[25]—such polls overstate their presence.[26] The more reliable voting data available from the Census Bureau indicate that college-educated voters made up only 29 percent of the electorate in 1994.[27] This was actually a smaller share of the active electorate than that claimed by voters with just a high school diploma (about 31 percent), and far smaller than the overall working-class share (about 71 percent).

Looking specifically at the forgotten majority, where almost all the 1992–94 decline in Democratic support occurred (black support for Democrats actually went up slightly), we find that the shift away from the Democrats was even more pronounced (see Chart 3.2). Forgotten majority men accounted for the sharpest declines. Democratic support among white men with only a high school education declined a whopping 20 points (to 37 percent); among white men with some college, it dropped 15 points (to 31 percent).

And it wasn't just the men. Working-class white women also deserted in droves—their support dropped 10 percentage points among both those with high school only and those with some college. Thus, to say that the fall-off in Democratic support was just about "angry white men"—a common assessment at the time—misses a good part of the picture.

What was true of the general electorate, moreover, was spectacularly true of Perot voters. Their ranks, as we showed earlier, were heavily dominated by the forgotten majority, and, indeed, forgotten majority Perot voters moved massively against the

CHART 3.2   Erosion of Democratic Congressional Support Among Whites, 1992–94

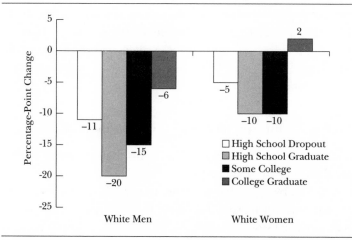

Source: Authors' analysis of 1992 VRS exit poll and 1994 VNS exit poll.

Democrats: down an astonishing 27 percentage points from 52 to 25 percent support. Moreover, Perot voters who voted Republican in 1994 were from groups under the most economic stress, with estimated post-1979 wage losses more than double those of Perot voters who voted Democratic.[28]

Finally, just to underscore the role of the forgotten majority as the true swing voters in this election, consider the difference among independent voters between the forgotten majority and college-educated whites. The support of forgotten majority independents for the Democrats plummeted 21 percentage points; that of college-educated white independents, a mere 5 points.

So, clearly, desertion of a hard-pressed forgotten majority was the real story behind the Democratic debacle in 1994—a pattern of desertion that is consistent with the story told earlier about Democratic presidential decline in the 1970s and 1980s. Just as with the Democratic presidential coalition, the decline of the

Democratic congressional coalition in 1994 was driven by the desertion of forgotten majority voters, particularly men, who expressed their pragmatic conservatism at the polling booth. In this sense, the 1994 election merely played out on a different stage the political feelings that these voters had expressed at the presidential level for decades. No more special dispensation for congressional Democrats, these voters seemed to be saying.

Alternative Interpretations of the 1994 Election

Our story of the 1994 election highlights the role of the forgotten majority and pragmatic conservatism. But there were other stories, too, being told at the time, from both the right and the left, and it is worth examining these to see if they can add much to our original story.

What About Ideology?

On the right, the most prominent explanation located the driving force of the pro-Republican surge in increased ideological conservatism among voters. This explanation built on the fact that the proportion of self-identified conservatives in the electorate increased over 1992 levels—from 30 to 37 percent—as did the rate at which they voted Republican—from 72 to 81 percent.[29] In addition, voter interest in, and apparent support for, the GOP's "Contract with America" was taken to mean that voters were embracing conservative ideology.

To begin with, as discussed in Chapter 2, the assumption that levels of self-identified conservatism really tap into levels of *ideological* conservatism, with its associated libertarianism on economic issues, is a questionable one. The 1992–94 change in conservative self-identification could easily have been one aspect of a rise in pragmatic, not ideological, conservatism. As we shall see, negative voter reaction to the Republicans' more ideological attempts to cut government after 1994 strongly supports this pragmatic conservatism hypothesis.

Second, the Contract with America was dominated by ideas that appealed to anti-government populism rather than to a hard-line, ideological conservatism. Proposals for term limits, the line item veto, cuts in congressional staff and perks, and a balanced budget amendment appealed to forgotten majority voters who were disgusted with government, but they didn't require these voters to endorse the rigorous anti-government ideology of a Newt Gingrich or Trent Lott.

Third, even granting that this shift was an ideological one, the proportion of conservatives in the 1994 electorate was not unusual by recent historical standards. The 1994 figure of 37 percent was only slightly higher than those recorded for the 1984 election (36 percent), the 1988 election (35 percent), and the 1990 election (34 percent).[30]

Finally, a 9-point shift away from the Democrats was not so large in the context of the 1994 election. We have already seen that anti-Democratic shifts among some demographic groups were as large as or larger than this figure. But even among groups defined by attitudes, the 9-point anti-Democratic shift among conservatives was dwarfed by shifts among other groups. Consider, for example, those defined by their attitude toward the economy: A 25-point shift against the Democrats occurred among those who thought the economy was not so good or poor (about three-fifths of the 1994 electorate), and a 36-point anti-Democratic shift occurred among those who thought their family situation was getting worse (about a quarter of the electorate).

In fact, when applied to the House vote in 1992 and 1994, statistical models that take self-reported "ideology," partisanship, and economic variables into account show little change in the magnitude of the effect of conservative self-identification.[31] The same models show much larger shifts in voting behavior associated with economic variables—such as family financial situation and assessment of the national economy (the effect of economic pessimism shifted from being quite pro-Democratic to being strongly anti-Democratic). They also show a large shift in the effect of partisanship, with independents much more likely to vote against the Democrats in 1994 than in 1992.[32] Indeed, after controlling for these other factors, we find no significant difference over 1992–94 in the relationship between conservatism and the House vote.[33]

This said, the increased weight of self-declared conservatism (whatever one's interpretation of such conservatism might be) among voters did play some role in the 1994 results. But the question is, How big a role, relative to other factors? Statistical procedures show that the shift in the share of conservatives in the electorate did make a contribution to the decline in the Democratic vote, but that contribution was less than one-fifth of the observed decline.[34] These procedures also show that the anti-Democratic shift among economic pessimists made a much larger contribution, and that an anti-Democratic shift among conservatives—that is, their increased rate of Republican voting—made no contribution at all.

What About Values?

Still another interpretation of the 1994 election focused on the role of values. Conservative political analyst Ben Wattenberg[35] traced the 1994 Democratic debacle to values issues like crime, welfare, and affirmative action,[36] arguing in general that "values matter most" and that economics matter relatively little in U.S. politics today (see the quote at the beginning of the chapter). This was a fashionable view in some quarters at the time—and even in the White House, if Wattenberg's account[37] of his telephone conversation with President Clinton is to be believed.

We argued earlier that this distinction between values and economics is artificial and should be discarded, since values always enter into voter decisions, no matter what the issue. It is more correct to say "values always matter" than "values matter most."

But what of the role of values *issues* as defined by Wattenberg? It is hard to deny that issues like crime and welfare had some influence in the 1994 election. They were on people's minds and much debated during the campaign. But evidence that these issues had a defining—or even large—effect on the 1994 election outcome is very hard to find. Consider specifically crime, the most central Wattenberg-style values issue in the 1994 campaign, and the one exit pollsters actually queried voters most extensively about.

To begin with, the exit polls showed that as many respondents cited the economy and jobs as motivations for their vote as cited crime. At a minimum, this suggests that concern over crime did not crowd out economic concerns. But more to the point, there is evidence that citing crime as an issue had no effect, independent of other factors, on voters' support for House candidates in 1994.[38] That is, those identifying crime as their key issue were no more likely to vote against the Democrats than those who did not. Of course, other values issues cited by Wattenberg might have revealed larger effects if the pollsters had asked about them. But the fact that crime, the highest-profile issue among his nominees, failed to show a discernible effect certainly arouses skepticism about this possibility.

Again, this is not to say that values played no role in the 1994 results—but we do believe that the values involved and the magnitude of their role are very imperfectly captured by a focus on hot-button issues like crime or welfare. For the reasons suggested earlier, we think it plausible that forgotten majority voters interpreted both the political and the economic situations in 1992–94 as inconsistent with their core values about work, responsibility, and fairness and punished the Democrats accordingly. In this sense, the election was certainly about values, but focus on Wattenberg's so-called values issues misses much else besides that.

What About Turnout?

A third interpretation of the 1994 election—this one identified more with the "left" than with the "right"—deserves comment—namely, that the root source of the Democrats' difficulty was their failure to turn out their base, particularly among poorer voters, black voters, and "hard-core" Democrats.

The first part of this get-out-the-base-vote argument is supported by evidence showing that turnout was relatively low among voters with less than $15,000 in household income (30 percent), compared to those with $50,000 or more in household income (59 percent)—a huge gap of 29 percentage points.[39] Moreover, the 30 percent figure for poor voters represented a drop of 5 percentage points from 1990, while the 59 percent figure for affluent voters represented a slight gain of 1 point. There is no question that there are very large, and growing, class differences in American voter turnout.[40] Nor is there much question that such differences hurt Democrats, whose support among the poorest voters—62 percent in 1994—is one of the few things on which they can rely.[41]

Even if we accept this evidence uncritically, however—and there are good reasons to believe the underlying data overestimate the decline in turnout among poor voters[42]—the changes in turnout over 1990–94 were too small to make a difference. Indeed, even if turnout among the poor had not fallen, but rather risen along with turnout among the affluent, the election results would have been virtually the same.[43] The Democrats received 46.5 percent of the two-party House vote in 1994 and trailed the

Republicans by more than 4.7 million votes.[44] If turnout among the poor had risen as much as turnout among the affluent, instead of declining, the Democrats would still have received only 47.1 percent of the vote and trailed the Republicans by more than 4.1 million votes.

If the first turnout argument concerns class, the second concerns race. Here, again, blacks are one of the few "reliably" Democratic constituencies, and low turnout among them has predictable bad effects on Democratic support. But applied to 1990–94, this argument also fails. For example, if black turnout had gone up as much as white turnout, instead of falling 2 percentage points, the Democrats would still have received just 46.9 percent of the House vote and trailed the Republicans by 4.3 million votes.

Combining arguments one and two, we find that it is possible to estimate the impact of declining turnout among both poor and black voters in the 1994 election. This is done by having black turnout rise as much as white turnout (instead of declining) and having white poor turnout rise as much as white affluent turnout (instead of declining). (The focus on the white poor is necessary to avoid double counting the many blacks who are poor.) This procedure shows little more effect than the first scenario of increased turnout among the poor. The cumulative impact still leaves the Democrats a little fewer than 4.1 million votes behind the Republicans, with roughly 47.1 percent of the two-party vote. These figures mean that, taken together, depressed turnouts among both blacks and the poor can account for only a trivial amount (8 percent) of the decline in the Democratic House vote. Thus, failure of the poor and blacks to turn out in the relative numbers they did in 1990 seems to have been only a minor factor in the 1994 Democratic defeat.[45] Even if they had turned out in such numbers, the results would have been substantially the same—perhaps a few less lost seats, but a thumping defeat nonetheless.

Finally, then, there is the argument about the failure of hard-core Democrats—regardless of their demographics—to rouse themselves relative to hard-core Republicans, some evidence for which was provided by a postelection poll conducted by the Democratic Leadership Council.[46] According to this poll, voters who voted in the 1992 election but did not turn out in 1994 (about 16 percent of the electorate) favored the Democrats by 12 percentage points—an outcome that implies a 58 percent support level[47] among those who would have voted for one of the two major parties. On the face of it, this seems compelling evidence for a rather large nonvoter effect.

But consideration of other data casts doubt on these findings. The 1994 edition of the National Election Studies (NES)—the mammoth biennial academic studies—found a substantially smaller pro-Democratic bias among those who voted in 1992 but did not vote in 1994 than was found in the Democratic Leadership Council survey. First, the NES data found that 40 percent of these nonvoters (about 6 percent of the total electorate), when handed a card with the names of the Democratic and Republican candidates, had no preference whatsoever between them. Second, of those who did express a preference—about 10 percent of the electorate—only 52 percent selected the Democrat.[48]

Confining our attention to only those nonvoters with definite preferences, and assuming half of these nonvoters had actually showed up at the polls in 1994—which would have created a turnout of about 43 percent, the highest off-year turnout since 1970 and an astonishing increase over 1990 of 7 percentage points—we find that the Democrats would still have received only 47.4 percent of the vote and continued to trail the Republicans by over 4 million votes. Thus, even a massive participation increase by these Democratic-leaning nonvoters would have made up only about 11 percent of the 1992–94 Democratic slide. Again, the implication is that, while depressed turnout among

Democratic supporters or groups may have been a factor in the 1994 Democratic defeat, it was not a major factor.

A final variant on all these arguments holds that problems in turnout were themselves concentrated in districts where Democrats lost seats and, hence, that national-level analyses of the sort made here cloak the effects of low participation. But according to political scientist Martin Wattenberg,[49] the degree of turnout drop-off (i.e., the difference between the turnouts of 1992 and 1994) in congressional districts bore no relationship at all with the swing toward the Republicans.[50] Here, too, the basic pattern of election results does not suggest a strong role for low turnout in the Democratic defeat.

We conclude that these alternative explanations—focusing on ideology, values, and turnout—do not call into question the basic story told in this chapter. Voter motivations in the election appear consistent with our focus on pragmatic—rather than ideological—conservatism and on core values around work, responsibility, and fairness rather than so-called values issues. Nor does a failure to get out the base Democratic vote of the Democratic base provide a convincing explanation of the election's outcome. We are back, in short, to forgotten majority voters, their pragmatic conservatism inflamed by political events and negative economic trends, punishing the Democratic party.

FOUR

Did the Forgotten Majority Matter in the 1990s? Part 2: The Elections of 1996 and 1998

[A]n army of soccer moms, driving to the polls in their mini-vans, . . . move[d] the Government to the center again.

—*New York Times,* NOVEMBER 10, 1996[1]

WE HAVE SEEN THAT THE NEW WHITE WORKING CLASS, America's forgotten majority, did not go away, at least in the early 1990s; indeed, it played a central role in both the 1992 and 1994 elections. But what of the elections of 1996 and 1998? These were the elections during which terms like *soccer mom* came into vogue and the national media seemed to lose interest in the white working class entirely. Did electoral demographics really change that much during these elections, or were the voters really the same but simply misinterpreted by the media?

We show in this chapter that the voters did not, in fact, change that much and that the forgotten majority continued to play a central role in both elections. We also show that, as political events unfolded and the economy continued to improve, the pragmatic conservatism of forgotten majority voters began to soften, creating possibilities for new political alignments. These possibilities, however, remained unrealized as both parties adopted strategies that did not take advantage of, or were actually contrary to, shifts in forgotten majority sentiment.

The 1996 Election

The Democratic Comeback

The Republican Revolution swept into Washington with Bill Clinton's approval ratings in the low 40s and Clinton losing to Bob Dole in trial presidential heats by 5 percentage points or more.[2] By the middle of 1996, Clinton claimed approval ratings in the low to mid-50s and was decisively beating Dole in trial heats by 15 to 20 points. Furthermore, Democrats were beating Republicans in generic congressional trial heats, while job approval of the Republican-dominated Congress was down 20 points from the spring of 1995. Finally, the public reported disagreeing more than agreeing with what the Republicans were doing in Congress (the percentage disagreeing was up 21 points since early 1995) and said they judged the Republican Congress more a failure than a success[3] (the percentage saying failure was up 14 points from early 1995). How did this dramatic turnaround occur?

The basic reason for the turnaround seems obvious in retrospect: Newt Gingrich and the congressional Republicans greatly overestimated their mandate. By attempting to move an agenda that weakened regulations on labor, pesticides, poisons in food, clean air, and clean water, that cut funding for EPA, OSHA, and other regulatory agencies, that eliminated the Commerce, Energy, and Education departments, and that reduced Medicare funding to provide capital gains tax cuts, the GOP was pushing a stringent anti-government crusade radically out of tune with the public's tastes. But the idea that they had overestimated their mandate was not so obvious at the time. Many observers seemed to believe as profoundly as the victorious Republicans that American voters had taken a distinctly ideological turn against government and would support such a wholesale deregulation and dismantling of government programs.

As argued earlier, this view was fundamentally mistaken. Rather than taking an ideological turn against government, voters turned on the Democrats because, from their common-sense, pragmatic perspective, government did not seem to be working well in the 1992–94 period: The priorities of government seemed at variance with their values, even as living standards continued to stagnate, other social problems failed to improve, and government expenditures continued apace. Given this assessment, it was time, reasoned the voters, to get rid of the Democrats and their style of government and to try something different.

But different in their view did not mean getting rid of, or even significantly trimming, government programs they liked, including environmental protection, education, and Medicare. Once it became apparent that such cuts would be included in the Republican drive to balance the budget—most infamously, cuts in Medicare that provided just enough money to fund tax cuts for business and the affluent—voters began to lose their enthusiasm for Republican-style budget balancing in particular and the Republican revolution in general. They massively opposed both the Republicans' Medicare cuts and their tax cuts, concluding that the GOP's main priority was to fund the tax cuts they wanted rather than to protect Medicare, and concurrently shifted toward a negative view of the Republican Congress.[4] This loss of enthusiasm set the stage for the Democratic comeback in late 1995.

This comeback was primarily driven by the Democrats' confrontation with Republican budget-balancing plans, rather than by Clinton's acquiescence to their overall goal of a balanced budget. Poll data convincingly show that Clinton's embrace of the goal of a balanced budget in June 1995 did relatively little to increase support for him and the Democrats (though it may have stabilized support levels at the time).[5] It was only later in the year, in the period shortly before the government shutdown on November 14, that the poll numbers really started turning in his and the Democrats' favor.[6] And this, of course, was the time when the White House finally joined congressional Democrats in a united-front opposition against the Republicans' plan. Evidently, confrontation was the driving force behind the Democrats' rise in popularity—not just a shift in thinking on the desirability of a balanced budget or the proclamation of the "end of the era of big government."

But while confrontation may have been key, it can still plausibly be argued that acceptance of the balanced budget played an important "table-setting" role in this period. At a minimum, it probably made it easier for voters to "hear" what the Democrats had to say about budget priorities, inasmuch as acceptance of the balanced budget removed the taint of fiscal irresponsibility from the party. Given this, could the Democrats have succeeded in their confrontations with Republican budgetary priorities without endorsing the balanced budget? Undoubtedly, it would have been harder to do so, but we'll never know for sure whether distaste for Republican extremism would have been enough for the public to ignore an unchanged Democratic fiscal stance.

What we do know is that embrace of the balanced budget was a further and important development in a fiscal-political logic that has effectively tied the Democrats' hands in terms of bold new initiatives to solve problems. As balancing the budget has led, through stages, to commitments to paying down the national debt and putting the Social Security surplus in a "lockbox," there has been very little room, either fiscally or politically, to argue for such initiatives. As we shall see, this lack of appealing initiatives has placed a rather low ceiling on Democratic support among the forgotten majority, even as their pragmatic conservatism has begun to abate—just enough to make some gains and, in terms of the congressional vote, to achieve rough parity with the Republicans. But not enough to build a new political majority.

At any rate, the most important reason the 1995 confrontation strategy actually succeeded is easily understood. Voters essentially "fired" the Democrats in 1994 because they had failed to make significant progress in solving the voters' economic and other problems. But the Republicans, instead of solving these problems, were now threatening to make things even worse! On top of continued stagnation in living standards, they were proposing to remove environmental safeguards, defund education programs, including school lunches, and, most important of all, cut Medicare, a critical part of most voters' economic security (current or future). And, to add insult to injury, they were proposing to reward the rich with new tax cuts.

This was simply unacceptable to most voters, especially most members of the forgotten majority, who concluded that the Republican Congress had been a failure. Indeed, what the Republicans succeeded in doing was to make themselves seem more of a threat to these voters' living standards and economic security than the Democrats and big government previously had seemed—fears that an inept Republican presidential campaign was never able to dispel. And, as long as this judgment remained in place, the Democrats and Bill Clinton continued to have the upper hand.

To add to the Republicans' woes, the Democrats received a strong boost from the economy beginning in early 1996. Productivity had started growing strongly at the beginning of the year, and, in the second quarter of the year, the overall economy grew at a stunning 6 percent annualized rate. In addition, real wages started inching upward in this period, after several years of going nowhere. The expansion, which had been tepid until this point, finally looked like it was going to deliver.

Reflecting these economic realities, public opinion took a marked turn toward the optimistic in the middle to late spring of 1996. For example, as late as April 1996, more than 7 in 10 Americans (72 percent) judged economic conditions as only fair or poor and just 27 percent thought they were excellent or good. By July, the excellent/good group had increased to 43 percent. And, by the eve of Clinton's reelection, the excellent/good group had reached 47 percent and the fair/poor group had declined to 52 percent, 20 percentage points below its level in April.

A similar trend can be observed in a polling question on whether economic conditions in the country were getting better or worse. In May 1996, more people still thought economic conditions were getting worse (49 percent) than thought they were getting better (39 percent). Just prior to Clinton's reelection, this relationship was reversed, such that more thought conditions were betting better (50 percent) than thought they were getting worse (38 percent).

Finally, people became markedly optimistic about their personal financial situation in the spring. Indeed, feelings that their financial situation had changed for the better in the past year—and would continue to change for the better in the next year—reached levels not seen since early 1990, right before the recession that brought down George Bush.

This surge of economic optimism, of course, was nothing but good news for the Democrats, the incumbent presidential party, especially since forgotten majority voters participated fully in the increased good feelings. There is no doubt it added to the lead that Clinton was already widening over Dole in early 1996.

The Democratic Triumph

As the campaign played itself out, Clinton maintained his advantage right through Election Day 1996 and became the first Democratic president to win two consecutive elections since Franklin Roosevelt.[7] Indeed, not only did he get reelected, he also bettered his showing over 1992, attracting 49 percent of the popular vote.

Most observers at the time credited Clinton's 1996 victory to his move to the "center," a move defined by his New Democrat–style emphasis on small government and family values. This stance, it was said, allowed him to reach relatively affluent, values-driven swing voters who delivered the election for him. Except for the first part of this claim—that he moved to the center—every other part of it is either inaccurate or radically incomplete.

As for moving to the center, this is one of those statements that says everything and nothing at the same time. Of course Clinton tried to be in the center, since two-party elections, by simple mathematics, are always about reaching voters in the center. So, since he won the election, he must have been in the center. The question is: Where was the center? This is the point at which the post-1996 conventional wisdom starts falling apart.

For example, take the issue of being a New Democrat. Polling data show that, during the period when Clinton built his decisive lead over Bob Dole in the polls, the percentage of the public who thought Clinton was a "new kind of Democrat" actually decreased, reaching the lowest levels of his presidency. Other polling data reinforce this point: In October 1994, right before the Democrats' November debacle, 44 percent of the public said

Clinton's approach to issues was liberal, 42 percent said it was moderate, and 9 percent said it was conservative. In October 1996, right before his successful reelection bid, the public's assessment was not just similar but identical: 44 percent liberal, 42 percent moderate, and 9 percent conservative.[8] Finally, another poll from late October of this year showed 51 percent of the public characterizing Clinton as a "tax and spend Democrat," compared to 39 percent who rejected this characterization.[9]

The key to resolving this paradox is recognizing that Clinton's political resurgence was based, as we saw earlier, on defense of Old Democrat programs (sometimes abbreviated, in the jargon of that election, as M2E2: Medicare, Medicaid, education, and the environment), as well as (somewhat closer to the election) on public perception of an improving economy. In contrast, New Democrat issues may have helped "inoculate" Clinton against Republican counterattacks, though they were not really the drivers of his resurgence. This interpretation is supported by exit poll results identifying the economy/jobs (21 percent), Medicare and Social Security (15 percent), and education (12 percent) as the key issues that moved voters into the Clinton column (three-fifths to three-quarters of voters who said these issues were their most important concerns voted for Clinton). These percentages compare very favorably to the numbers of voters motivated by New Democrat–style issues: Just 40 percent of crime/drugs voters (7 percent of the electorate) and only 27 percent of budget deficit voters (12 percent of the electorate) voted for Clinton.

A postelection survey conducted by Stanley Greenberg for the Campaign for America's Future (CAF) found similar motivations among Clinton voters. Almost three-fifths (59 percent) of Clinton voters in this survey—even more among forgotten majority Clinton voters—cited his support of domestic programs (education, Medicare, and the environment), compared to fewer than one-third (31 percent) who cited his support of New Democrat–style positions (welfare reform, anti-crime measures, balanced budget, and moderation).

Another clear demonstration of the relative importance of M2E2 came from a postelection poll conducted by, interestingly enough, the Democratic Leadership Council (DLC), the progenitors of the New Democrat idea. That poll asked voters several questions on what "this election was about." The clear winner: "preserving Medicare, Medicaid, education, and the environment" over such New Democrat favorites as "expanding opportunity, responsibility, and working together as a community" and "ending old-style liberalism and bringing the Democratic Party into the mainstream."

These data suggest that Clinton may have moved to the center, and that doing so helped win him the election, but also, more substantively, that the center had at least as much to do with not-so-new Democrat issues (protecting Medicare, Medicaid, education, and the environment) as with New Democrat issues. This is not to deny that some New Democrat issues may have helped Clinton add to his lead at the margin, or may have set the table for him to pursue his advantage on other issues. But the real point here is that these issues did not create the basic advantage that Clinton rode to his reelection. Instead, his stalwart defense of M2E2 should be credited, especially among forgotten majority voters. He was able to tap commitment among these and other voters to the basics of the welfare state and connect to the widespread sentiment that the Republicans were extreme and only likely to make things worse, if allowed to have their way. Combined with rapidly improving public perceptions of the economy in the months immediately prior to the election, this political stance gave him an insuperable advantage in the election campaign.

Indeed, given the rapid improvement in public views of the economy, the highly popular defense of M2E2, and the weakness of Bob Dole as a Republican standard-bearer, the real mystery of the election was the Democrats' failure to win more than 49 percent of the vote in such a highly favorable climate. We can solve this mystery by locating where Clinton did and did not find increased support.

As we will see, the forgotten majority is once again at center stage in both these instances. That is, not only Clinton's increased support, but also his inability to muster a majority of the popular vote, turns out to be driven by forgotten majority voters—just different segments in each case.

The Rise of the Soccer Mom?

> Soccer Mom: . . . The bio-political successor to the Silent Majority, Reagan Democrat, Angry White Male and other swing-vote icons of elections past.
>
> —*Boston Globe*, OCTOBER 30, 1996[10]

Perhaps the most memorable theme of the 1996 election was the enshrinement of affluent suburbanites, particularly the now-legendary "soccer moms," as the new swing voters in American politics. New Democrats—who started life as a movement to recapture whites of modest means for the Democratic party—were prominent subscribers to this thesis and its direct implication: that Clinton's electoral success in 1996 was attributable to the great inroads he made among these new swing voters.

This view was widely echoed in the media and quickly congealed as the conventional wisdom on the election (see the quote at the beginning of this chapter). There is one slight problem, however: To the extent this army of soccer moms was envisioned as upscale and college-educated, actual data on the election don't support this interpretation. Instead, they suggest that the key change for Clinton in 1996 was increased support among the working class, particularly the forgotten majority.

CHART 4.1   Increase in Democratic Presidential Support, 1992–96

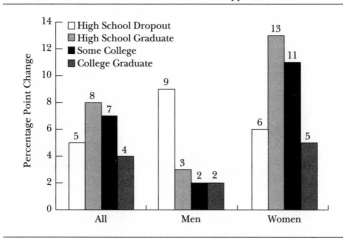

Source: Author's analysis of 1992 VRS exit poll and 1996 VNS exit poll.

Polling data from the election[11] reveal that voters with a high school diploma and voters with some college increased their support of Clinton by 8 and 7 percentage points, respectively (see Chart 4.1). In contrast, college-educated voters increased their support by about half as much (4 points). Given these figures, and the fact that working-class voters far outnumber their college-educated counterparts,[12] it is not surprising that working-class voters accounted for more than three-quarters of Clinton's overall increase in support.[13]

The increase in working-class Clinton support was driven in turn by a strong increase in Hispanic support (up 11 points among a heavily working-class population) and, more important, a solid increase in support among members of the much more numerous forgotten majority: They increased their support of Clinton by 5 points, while their college-educated, far more affluent counterparts managed an increase of less than 3 points.

CHART 4.2   Increase in Democratic Presidential Support Among Whites, 1992–96

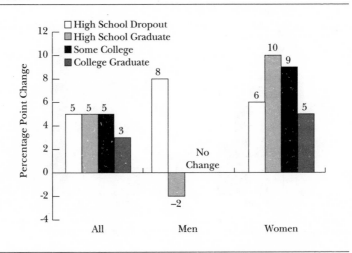

Source: Authors' analysis of 1992 VRS exit poll and 1996 VNS exit poll.

It was also widely noted that Clinton's increased support in 1996 came overwhelmingly from women. And it is true that Clinton's support increased by 9 points among women, but only 2 points among men, thereby widening the gender gap considerably in his favor. Is there any contradiction between this observation and the one about the centrality of the forgotten majority? Not at all: Together they simply imply that forgotten majority women played the key role in Bill Clinton's reelection. For example, exit poll data (see Chart 4.2) show that Clinton's success among women voters was driven by particularly strong rises among white women high school graduates (up 10 points) and white women with some college (up 9 points). Indeed, the rise in Clinton's support among these two groups is really what drove the widening gender gap.

CHART 4.3   Change in Democratic Vote for President by Key Demographics Among Whites, 1992–96

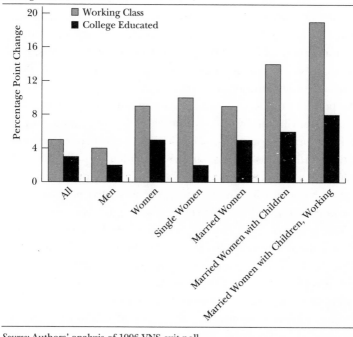

Source: Authors' analysis of 1996 VNS exit poll.

These findings suggest that the role of women voters, defined by such characteristics as marriage and children rather than by class, should be carefully evaluated. This is particularly the case with the role of "soccer moms" in that election, insofar as we can define them. The first thing to note is that single white women—not usually thought of as soccer moms—actually increased their support of Bill Clinton just as much as married white women did (by 7 percentage points).

The second thing to note is the strong influence of class. Married forgotten majority women increased their support of Clinton by almost twice as much (see Chart 4.3) as their more upscale, college-educated counterparts (9 points versus 5 points). And looking just at married women with children, approaching the conventional definition of soccer mom, we find that the class split is even more lopsided. Forgotten majority mothers increased their support of Clinton by 14 points, compared to just 6 points among white college-educated mothers. Further refinements of the soccer mom formula only underscore the point: Forgotten majority employed mothers increased their support of Clinton by 19 points, their college-educated counterparts by only 8 points. Nor does it change the pattern of results significantly to look just at suburban women or politically independent women or even suburban independent women with these characteristics: In each case, the forgotten majority tilt to Clinton's increased support remains at a high level.

This analysis suggests that emphasizing the role of soccer moms obscures more than clarifies the results of the 1996 election. Not only did single women in the forgotten majority increase their support of Clinton just as much as married women, but, within the ranks of those women who most closely fit the definition of soccer moms, the move toward Clinton was heavily dominated by forgotten majority women. This finding directly calls into question the 1996 election stereotype of affluent, Volvo-driving suburban mothers as the new Democratic voters. Instead, these new Democratic voters were more likely to be moms driving Cavaliers, struggling to get by economically, and worrying that family financial meltdown could be right around the corner—in other words, members in good standing of America's forgotten majority.

Wage and income data illustrate the economic strains on these voters at the time of that election. Through the end of 1996, the economic expansion had failed to lift real wages and household incomes for forgotten majority women above levels attained in 1989, the last pre-recession year (still down 3 percent). These data bring the women most responsible for reelecting Bill Clinton into sharper focus. And it is a very different, more economically stressed portrait than that painted by media accounts at the time. What it does not do, however, is explain the gender gap in forgotten majority support—why it was women rather than men in this group who shifted into Clinton's column. Indeed, given the long-term economic difficulties experienced by these women, why did they support the incumbent president?

For three reasons. The first is that women and men had (and have) different attitudes toward the role of government, particularly with regard to social spending—that is, spending on just the kind of programs that were centerpiece issues in the campaign. While women distrusted government at roughly the same level as men, they were more likely to be believers in government's essential role in providing social services like health care and education. They were also more likely than men to expect the government to make job availability and a wholesome social and family environment a priority. Since Clinton's campaign became defined so strongly by his defense of M2E2, women had more reason than men to overlook their basic distrust of government and long-term economic difficulties and to move into Clinton's column. And the additional definition of his campaign by small-scale government regulation proposals to strengthen the family and social environment area (the v-chip, school uniforms, extending family and medical leave, etc.) probably reinforced this special appeal to women.

The second reason strengthened the first. Forgotten majority women had especially high levels of anxiety about the future. For example, in the Greenberg/CAF survey, these women exhibited real fear about their future. Seventy-one percent were very concerned about being unable to afford health care when a family member was sick, 61 percent were very concerned with not having enough money for retirement, 60 percent feared their children would not have good job opportunities, and 54 percent were concerned about being unable to save enough money to put a child through college. Only black[14] voters exhibited higher levels of concern about their future.

Given their high levels of anxiety about economic problems, it follows that forgotten majority women would support anyone promising to mitigate these problems. Combined with their greater openness to government programs in these areas, this factor goes a long way toward explaining why these women swung so heavily in Clinton's direction.

The third reason for Clinton's exceptional success with forgotten majority women is that, despite their levels of anxiety and their long-term economic difficulties, these women did experience tangible economic improvement in the period immediately prior to the election. This improvement led to improved short-term economic perceptions that, in turn, made it easier for these voters to support the incumbent president. How did forgotten majority women improve their economic situation even while they continued to experience wage stagnation? Over several decades when wages had been going nowhere, they had responded by increasing their working hours, while more of their household members worked.[15] These mechanisms for maintaining and possibly raising family living standards were facilitated by continued job creation and relatively low unemployment in the period leading up to the election.

The success of these mechanisms is demonstrated by the rising household incomes of forgotten majority women in 1994–96. For example, the median household income of these women went up 4 percent during this interval, even as their wages actually declined by 1 percent. This improvement did not erase their post-1989 income losses, as we mentioned earlier, but it was enough to produce a substantially more positive attitude toward the incumbent and his stewardship of the economy. In conjunction with their concerns about preserving social spending and long-term economic security, this explains, we believe, the sharp swing toward Clinton among forgotten majority women.

But it is important to stress the words *in conjunction:* Increased economic optimism, by itself, would have done little to explain why these women, in particular, moved so strongly in Clinton's direction between 1992 and 1996. For example, forgotten majority men, whose support for Clinton didn't budge over the two elections, were much more optimistic than their female counterparts at the time of the election. So economic optimism must be combined with other factors to explain why Clinton did particularly well among forgotten majority women.

This discussion bring us back to the central mystery of the 1996 election. If voters were so optimistic about the economy—and issues and relative candidate appeal also heavily favored them—why couldn't the Democrats do better than 49 percent? In particular, why couldn't Clinton do better among forgotten majority men who were actually more optimistic than their female counterparts?

The answer lies in the continued undertow on Democratic support from pragmatic conservatism, which was exceptionally strong among men in the new white working class. Polled right after the election,[16] three-fifths of these voters still expressed general agreement with the sentiment "the less government the better." For forgotten majority men, short-term economic optimism was evidently not sufficient to cause them to disregard—or even substantially modify—their view that government did not share their values and could not be a positive force for solving their longer-term economic and other problems. Indeed, given how poorly this group fared between 1992 and 1996—for example, the median wage of forgotten majority men was still 10 percent lower at the end of 1996 than in 1989 (18 percent lower than in 1979)—their failure to progress economically probably reinforced their suspicions about the efficacy of government. These suspicions, in turn, helped lower Democratic support to levels considerably below those necessary for a dominant electoral coalition.

Who Rejoined the House Democrats?

If a close examination of the presidential election results fails to support the "soccer mom" interpretation of Clinton's success, what of the congressional election results? Mark Penn, the New Democrat pollster for both President Clinton and the DLC, argued that the House Democrats, "egged on by the labor unions, . . . invested heavily in wooing the so-called 'downscale' voters . . . and failed to join Clinton in . . . demonstrating fiscal moderation. . . . Had the Democrats moved with the President toward more mainstream positions, they would have retaken the House."[17] Perhaps here the soccer mom interpretation applies in a negative sense: Forgotten majority voters did not play a central role, despite Democrats' efforts to reach them, and the failure to reach soccer moms—with New Democrat–style politics—was the real story. A close examination of actual data on the election, however, indicates that such an interpretation is oversimplified in some respects and just plain wrong in others.

To begin with, the House Democrats received 49 percent of the popular vote, about the same proportion as the Republicans and also about the same proportion as Clinton in the presidential contest. Thus, Clinton, despite his highly touted New Democrat approach, did not succeed in outpolling the House Democrats. In fact, neither achieved a popular majority. In addition, Clinton did not actually reach many soccer moms, at least in the upscale sense, but was bolstered instead by an infusion of support from forgotten majority women. Finally, analysis of

CHART 4.4   Change in Democratic Congressional Support, 1994–96

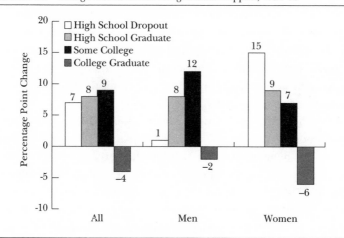

Source: Authors' analysis of 1994 and 1996 VNS exit polls.

which voters rejoined the congressional Democrats—they increased their share of the popular vote for the House by 3 percentage points over 1994—reveals, once again, the central role of the forgotten majority.

Exit poll data show that the increase in the Democratic House vote was even more dominated by the working class than the increase in Clinton's support. Recall that, in 1994, the shift away from the Democrats was concentrated exclusively among the working class. The change in 1996 was almost a mirror image (see Chart 4.4). The increase in Democratic support was also confined to the working class, especially high school graduates (up 8 points) and those with some college (up 9 points), while support actually declined among those with a college education (down 4 points).

This increase in working-class Democratic House support was, in turn, driven by a sharp increase in Hispanic support (up 11 points among an overwhelmingly working-class population) and, more significantly, by a strong increase in forgotten majority support (up 8 points over 1994). Breaking these data down further by gender shows that House Democrats, in contrast to Clinton, made strong gains among forgotten majority men, not just women. Indeed, House Democratic gains among forgotten majority men were actually greater than among their female counterparts (9 versus 7 points).

Why the swing back toward congressional Democrats among the forgotten majority? Much of the explanation lies in the same factor that benefited Clinton in 1996: the perception that the Republican plans for the budget (M2E2) were a greater problem than the Democrats' attachment to "big government." More generally, many of the forgotten majority voters who, in 1994, targeted the Democrats and government as the agent of living standards and related problems concluded, by 1996, that the Republicans and their blanket hostility even to useful government programs were an even greater threat to their struggle to get by. Thus, these voters, including a good number of the men who had deserted so heavily in 1994, swung back toward the Democrats, despite their continued deep suspicion of government and continued wage and income problems. In addition, of course, the House Democrats benefited from the economy's relatively strong performance as the election neared—a factor that began to take the edge off some of these problems.

If the demographic part of the soccer mom interpretation doesn't hold, what of the New Democrat part? Did the Democrats fail to take back the House because they didn't embrace fiscal moderation and school uniforms? Perhaps, though our analysis of the issues basis of Clinton's success does not suggest New Democrat issues were that powerful as electoral motivations. Moreover, the congressional Democrats did, in fact, loyally promulgate the president's basic message and adopt a "Families First" legislative agenda that was notable for its moderation, not militancy.

There are also other, more plausible suspects for the Democrats' failure to do better. These include (1) the Democratic fund-raising scandal at the end of the campaign, which hurt their congressional candidates; (2) the tremendous counterpunch by business-backed Republicans in the final stages of the campaign, as business went on to outspend labor by 7 to 1 ($242 million to $35 million); and (3) bipartisan cooperation with House Republicans, including the passing of the welfare bill, the Kennedy-Kassebaum health insurance bill, and the minimum wage bill, which reduced negative feelings about the Republican Congress.

So neither the demographic nor the New Democrat part of the soccer mom interpretation seems a convincing explanation for the House Democrats' shortcomings. In addition, by essentially claiming that Clinton built a new base, while the House Democrats didn't,[18] the soccer mom argument thoroughly misrepresents the nature of these shortcomings. Looking back to 1992, we recall that Clinton got 43 percent of the vote in 1992, while House Democrats got 54 percent. Thus, the House Democrats, unlike Bill Clinton, didn't need to build a new base; they just needed to keep the old one—something they failed to do in 1994, but made progress toward regaining in 1996.

The same holds true when we look at the House Democrats' base among specific groups such as youth and women. For example, they got 55 percent of the women's vote in 1992 and 1996, perfectly adequate for controlling Congress under most circumstances, and actually a percentage point higher than Clinton received in 1996 even after his large increase in women's support. Similarly, the House Democrats polled 55 percent of the youth vote in 1996, 2 points higher than Clinton despite his much-emphasized popularity among this group.

So, the House Democrats' "failure" to increase their support—to build a new base—over 1992 levels was hardly a sign of weakness. In fact, if their support levels had remained steady across all demographic groups between 1992 and 1996, they'd have controlled Congress quite easily in the 1996 election. The real problem was where their support fell in 1994 and didn't recover to 1992 levels. And the most important place here was among forgotten majority men. Support among forgotten majority men fell 18 points in 1994 and, despite recovering by 9 points in 1996, was still 9 points below 1992 levels in that election. This is in contrast to forgotten majority women, whose support fell by 9 points in 1994 but rose by 7 points in 1996, almost making it back to 1992 levels.

Thus, the House Democrats' real challenge coming out of the 1996 election was to increase their support among forgotten majority men[19] from 44 percent to closer to what it had been in 1992: 53 percent. The soccer mom/New Democrat issues approach was hardly the obvious approach to meeting this challenge, given the election results just reviewed. After all, even President Clinton, the New-Democrat-in-Chief, got only 38 percent support among this group in 1996—6 points lower than the supposed Democratic dinosaurs in the House!

From 1996 to the 1998 Election

Broadly speaking, three general trends affected politics from 1996 to 1998, all of them breaking in the Democrats' favor. First, there was the vigorous performance of the economy: Not only did strong overall economic growth continue (over 4 percent real growth in both 1997 and 1998), but real wages rose considerably and across the board—over 2 percent per year at the median, even better for lower-wage workers below the median, and fully affecting both forgotten majority men and women. Combined with—and related to—low and falling unemployment and negligible inflation, this was a very favorable environment for the typical worker, whether within or outside the forgotten majority, probably the best since 1973. In addition, the strong economic growth produced a stream of government revenue that, by late 1997, actually wiped out the budget deficit and implied large future surpluses if growth continued.

Reflecting these good economic times, feelings of economic optimism continued to rise. While 52 percent of voters considered the economy only fair or poor at the time of Clinton's reelection, by March 1998 only 34 percent shared this negative view. Similarly, just prior to Clinton's reelection, half thought economic conditions were getting better compared to 38 percent who thought they were getting worse. By March 1998, those who thought conditions were getting better (69 percent) vastly outnumbered those who thought they were getting worse (21 percent).

Even more tellingly, two March 1998 Gallup poll questions that asked respondents to assess their personal financial situation—recent past and short-term future—showed the most optimistic readings since the questions were first asked in September 1976. Finally, the Conference Board's June 1998 reading of its consumer-confidence index reached the highest level (137.6) recorded since June 1969.

While these indicators of economic optimism all subsided somewhat in the latter part of 1998, they remained at very high levels through the November election, both in general and among the forgotten majority, reflecting continuing excellent economic conditions. Adding to the natural advantage this created for the Democrats as the incumbent party were two public opinion trends that broke in their favor.

The first of these was an increasingly strong advantage for Democrats on a wide range of economic issues. This was because levels of anxiety about health and retirement security, educational opportunity, and other long-range problems had been tempered somewhat by the economic optimism of the two-year period, though hardly eliminated. Coupled with perceived Republican callousness about these problems, the result was a widening gap in public preferences in favor of the Democrats. Indeed, by the eve of the election, Democrats were enjoying huge advantages ranging from 21 to 33 percentage points on issues from health care to Social Security to education.

The second public opinion trend was the elimination of the Republican advantage on social issues, if not a turnaround to a slight Democratic advantage. No longer able to use crime, welfare, and abortion to paint the Democrats as excessively tolerant, Republicans turned to the Lewinsky scandal to revive their fortunes in the social realm. As everyone now knows, the strategy backfired as the American people demonstrated far more tolerance of Clinton's personal misbehavior than the Republicans had hoped. (This tolerance, it should be noted, is entirely consistent with the increasing social liberalism of the population documented in Chapter 2.) Republicans proved to be profoundly out of touch with the zeitgeist in this area and, as a result, reaped no small measure of ill will among voters for their perceived extremism in impeaching and then attempting to remove Clinton from office.

Together, these three trends hurt the Republicans. Replacing the social wedge issues that used to benefit the GOP, there emerged instead a set of new wedge issues that were basically economic—Social Security, Medicare, education, and health care. And the continued surge of the economy and economic optimism deprived the Republicans of veins of potential discontent to mine. In fact, the reverse was happening. With work being rewarded in a way that hadn't been seen in decades, the pragmatic conservatism of the forgotten majority was softening considerably and pent-up demand for government action in key areas was emerging.

The 1998 Election

Riding the economic and public opinion trends just described, the Democrats were able to turn in a strong performance in the

1998 election, though, as we shall see, they continued to have big problems with forgotten majority voters. Contrary to virtually all predictions, they held their own in the Senate and the nation's governorships and actually picked up 5 seats in the House. Moreover, their gains in the House defied historical precedent: In this century, the average loss for the president's party six years into a president's tenure has been 38 seats. Even taking into account the Republicans' 52-seat pickup in 1994, the Democrats still did well over the course of the two Clinton midterm elections: 47 seats lost versus the historical average of 62.

The bad news for the Democrats was that they were still a very weak party below the level of the presidency. Following the 1998 election, Democratic strength below the presidential level remained (with one exception: the eightieth Congress of 1947–49) at its lowest ebb since the Great Depression and the advent of the New Deal. Just six years before, when Bill Clinton had first gained the presidency, the Democrats had controlled the House, 258 to 176; the Senate, 57 to 43; and the nation's governorships, 30 to 18. After the 1998 election, the *Republicans* controlled the House, 223 to 211; the Senate, 55 to 45; and the nation's governorships by a lopsided 31 to 17.

The good news for the Democrats in this election is not difficult to explain in light of the strong economy and their emerging advantages on key issues. Consistent with this explanation, exit polls showed that voters who selected health care as their key issue (6 percent of the electorate) preferred the Democrats by 69 to 31 percent; those who selected education—the most of any issue (20 percent)—preferred the Democrats by 67 to 33 percent; those who selected the economy/jobs (14 percent) preferred them by 65 to 35 percent; and those who selected Social Security (12 percent) preferred them by 59 to 41 percent (see Table 4.1). Reports from around the country suggested that it

TABLE 4.1   Democratic Support, by Issue That Mattered Most in House Vote, 1998

Percent of Voters Selecting Issue	Issue	Democratic Support[1]
6	Health care	69
20	Education	67
14	Economy/Jobs	65
12	Social Security	59
5	Clinton/Lewinsky matter	44
13	Taxes	29
18	Moral and ethical standards	16

[1] Based on two-party vote.
Source: Authors' analysis, 1998 VNS exit poll.

was indeed these issues that Democrats emphasized over and over again in their campaign commercials.

The Hole in the Democratic Electorate

The bad news for the Democrats in the 1998 election bears a bit more explanation. It brings us back to the subject of this book—the forgotten majority. Despite the strong economy and the stunning issue advantages just outlined, forgotten majority voters remained remarkably tepid about the Democrats in the 1998 election.

For example, Democratic House support among whites without a high school diploma remained 12 points lower than it was in 1992, 10 points lower among whites with a high school diploma only, and 8 points lower among whites with some college (see Chart 4.5). In contrast, support was only 3 points lower among both whites with a college degree only and whites with a postgraduate education. Moreover, this pattern was replicated in the short term, with the Democrats losing substantial ground between 1996 and 1998 among forgotten majority voters at all education levels,

CHART 4.5   Change in Democratic Support Among Whites, by Education
Group, 1992–98

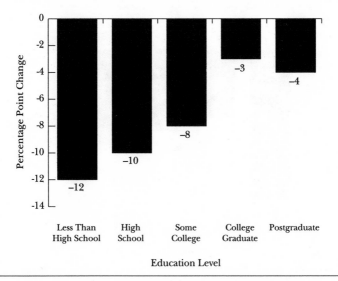

Source: Authors' analysis of 1992 VRS exit poll and 1998 VNS exit poll.

losing only modestly among white college graduates, and gaining
slightly among whites with a postgraduate education.

Indeed, the Democrats were in such sad shape with the forgotten majority in 1998 that they received only 42 percent of the
vote in the heart of the white working class: those with a high
school degree or some college. The fact that these voters consti-
tute over four-fifths of the forgotten majority suggests just how
tenuous the Democratic position with this group was.

Breaking these data down by gender shows that Democratic
losses in the 1992–98 period were much heavier among the forgotten majority than among the college-educated for both men
and women. In addition, the magnitudes of decline among forgotten majority men and women were surprisingly similar, with the

CHART 4.6   Change in Democratic Support Among Whites, by Income Group, 1992–98

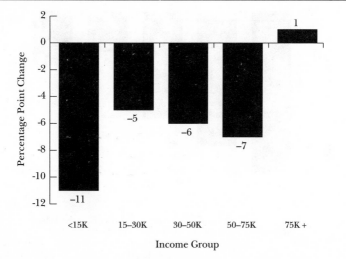

Source: Authors' analysis of 1992 VRS exit poll and 1998 VNS exit poll.

exception of white male high school graduates, who reduced their Democratic support by an amazing 14 percentage points, compared to "only" a 6-point decline among their female counterparts.

To flesh out this picture, recall that the overwhelming proportion of the forgotten majority—more than four-fifths—have household incomes below $75,000. Between 1992 and 1998, the Democrats lost substantial support among whites in all income categories below $75,000 and slightly gained ground with affluent voters above $75,000 (see Chart 4.6). Indeed, among whites in the moderate $30,000–$75,000 range, where the typical white is located, the Democrats were at an astonishingly low 41 percent support level in the 1998 election, having lost 6 points in the $30,000–$50,000 category and 7 points in the $50,000–$75,000 category over the six-year period. The data for 1996 and 1998 were also consistent with this pattern, showing a particularly healthy increase in Democratic support among affluent whites.

Where the Democrats Lost Seats in the 1990s

It is possible that these national exit poll results overemphasize the role of the forgotten majority in Democratic congressional decline and that other demographic groups were more important in individual Congressional Districts (CDs) lost by the Democrats. A look at the districts where the Democrats lost seats in the 1992–98 period, however, simply confirms the central importance of forgotten majority voters.

Overall, Census data on districts lost by the Democrats indicate that the 1990 population in such districts averaged 81 percent white,[20] 83 percent working class,[21] 40 percent suburban, and 38 percent rural and had a median income of just over $36,000[22] (see Table 4.2). Even if we make allowances for demographic and economic change since 1990[23] (when these Census data were collected) and the fact that working-class voters are less likely to vote than college-educated voters, these data suggest that the typical voter in the districts where the Democrats lost seats between 1992 and 1998 did not remotely resemble the affluent, college-educated suburbanite enshrined by the conventional wisdom as the key swing voter. Instead, the typical voter in these districts was a forgotten majority voter of modest income (below the national median) who may or may not have lived in the suburbs.

The forgotten majority part of this description makes especially good sense since (1) most districts in the nation are overwhelmingly populated by working-class voters and (2) most districts in the country contain big majorities of white voters and the Democrats continue to control—and control quite safely—

TABLE 4.2 Lost Democratic Seats, by Key Demographics, 1992–98

	Percent				Median
	White[1]	Working-Class[2]	Suburban	Rural[3]	Household Income[4]
DP Seats Lost, 1992–98[5]	81	83	40	38	$36,188
South	76	85	37	48	32,479
Non-South	85	80	42	29	39,678
All DP Seats	66	80	47	16	38,969
South	60	83	38	27	33,171
Non-South	69	79	50	12	41,382
All GOP Seats	82	80	52	28	41,561
South	79	81	50	31	37,647
Non-South	84	79	54	25	44,064
All Seats	74	80	50	22	40,301
South	71	82	45	29	35,784
Non-South	76	79	52	18	42,662

[1] Non-Hispanic white.

[2] Lacking a four-year college degree, based on those persons 18 years or older.

[3] Defined as non-metropolitan areas.

[4] In 1998 dollars.

[5] Seat was Democratic in 103rd Congress and is Republican in 106th Congress.

Note: All demographics reflect information collected by the 1990 Census.

Source: Author's analysis of 1990 Census data, STF 1D/3D.

62 out of 64 seats that are at least one-third minority. Therefore, the seats they were likely to lose—and did lose—were going to be seats where working-class and white voters are strong majorities.

As was widely reported, most of these Democratic losses took place in the South. Is it the case, then, that Democratic losses in the Midwest and West (where almost all of the rest of the losses took place) took place in substantially different districts and that southern losses were actually driving these figures? Not according to the Census data: The average Democratic loss outside the South took place in a district that was 85 percent white and still 80 percent working class. In addition, the median income in these nonsouthern districts, while closer to the national median, was still about $3,000 below the median[24] in all districts outside the South and over $4,000 below the median in all nonsouthern districts controlled by the Republicans.

The one way in which lost districts outside the South really differed is that they were much less rural. Nonsouthern districts lost by the Democrats averaged just 29 percent rural, in contrast to 38 percent rural in all districts they lost and 48 percent rural in districts they lost in the South. However, even with this difference the typical voter in these nonsouthern districts lost by the Democrats was still more likely to be urban or rural than suburban.

Indeed, the only area in which the affluent suburban swing voter seems to be at all typical is in the Northeast, where lost Democratic districts averaged over three-quarters suburban, with median incomes exceeding $48,000. But this was an area in which the Democrats, on net, actually gained seats over the 1992–98 period, losing just 4 seats and picking up 8.

In contrast, in the Midwest, where the Democrats lost (overall) the most seats in any region save the South, the typical lost district was 90 percent white, 83 percent working class, and just 36 percent suburban, with a modest median income of about $36,500. Again, such findings underscore the differences between the true swing voters driving congressional Democratic decline and the stereotype promulgated by the conventional wisdom.

Conclusion: The Challenge of the Forgotten Majority

The 1996 and 1998 election results exemplify the challenge facing both parties. The Democrats responded to their 1994 setback by dismantling the new synthesis that initially elected Bill Clinton. In so doing, they inoculated themselves against a series of Republican attacks that mobilized pragmatic conservatism against them. But the other side of this repositioning was a severe limit on the kinds of government action and spending that could make a convincing dent in the problems of the forgotten majority, thereby potentially winning it away from pragmatic conservatism and consolidating it in the Democratic column.

The 1997 budget deal and its aftermath only deepened this contradiction in Democratic strategy. In order to produce a future balanced budget, the deal mandated unrealistically low levels of domestic spending that would result in future real cuts in already-existing programs and leave no fiscal room for new ones. Then, when projected budget surpluses started appearing way ahead of schedule in late 1997, the Clinton administration, by pledging to "save Social Security first," in effect took these surpluses off the table. In so doing, it ensured that the surpluses couldn't be used either for tax cuts (which the Republicans wanted) or for wasteful new spending that could typecast the Democrats as big spenders again. But it also ensured that there was very little money available for new initiatives no matter how worthy or how potentially popular with a forgotten majority whose pragmatic conservatism was beginning to erode. Instead, the surpluses were allocated to paying down the national debt, until such time as the retirement system's long-term solvency problems were solved.

This situation has left the Democrats with little else to do other than defend "Old Democrat" social insurance programs like Social Security and Medicare and emphasize relatively modest differences between themselves and the Republicans on issues like education and HMO regulation. Such a stance has generally played in the Democrats' favor—reflecting the public opinion trends outlined earlier—and has helped turnout the Democrats' union/minority base; but it clearly has not succeeded in generating enthusiasm among most forgotten majority voters. For this reason, the Democrats remain—ironically, since New Democrat–style politics was supposed to produce the exact reverse—a party utterly dependent on old issues and heavy turnout of their old base, simply to break even. But their bid for a majority coalition has been stymied.

The Republicans' challenge is to hold onto their 1998 dominance of the forgotten majority and even expand it back to 1994 levels. Or, lacking such success, they need to break into the Democrats' strongly supportive union/minority base, which gives the Democrats a lock on a substantial portion of the electorate. But a lesson of the 1994–98 period is that neither a fierce anti-government program nor an intolerant social conservatism appeals to the forgotten majority on the level needed by the Republicans for a majority coalition. And certainly neither appeals to the Democratic base. Instead, forgotten majority voters appear interested in genuine solutions to their problems—solutions that may require government action and spending on a level seemingly inconsistent with the Republicans' basically anti-government stance. Yet to reject, or substantially modify, the anti-government approach that characterizes the party would endanger the very pragmatic conservatism that the party depends on for support with the forgotten majority.

The results are the now-familiar partisan stalemate and policy paralysis that characterize contemporary American politics. Both parties are, in essence, afraid to move very far off their current stances, yet both parties can't build majority coalitions without doing so. In the next chapter, we examine the problems of coalition building in more detail and discuss how the mobilization of the forgotten majority figures in the possible futures of American politics.

FIVE

Does the Forgotten Majority Still Matter?

In most recent election cycles, Democrats, powerfully aided by teachers and other unions and the growing political activism of Latinos and African-Americans, have developed voter identification and turnout tools more efficient than Republicans and their allies in either business or the religious conservative movement have deployed. The Democrats could win the voter mobilization war.

—DAVID BRODER, *Washington Post*, JANUARY 5, 2000[1]

WE HAVE ESTABLISHED THE CENTRAL ROLE played by the forgotten majority in 1990s electoral politics. But what of the future? Can either party move forward without the forgotten majority? If so, how? If not, why not? And, regardless of the current situation, will demographic change—the decline of whites as a percentage of the population and the increasing prevalence of people with a college degree—rapidly diminish the impact of the forgotten majority? This chapter answers these questions, in the process clarifying the political challenges facing both parties—and any third party as well.

To test whether either major party can move forward without the forgotten majority, we first separate union voters from other voters. Even among the forgotten majority, members of union households[2] remain broadly Democratic—voting 56 percent Democratic in the 1998 House elections, for example, as compared to 39 percent among nonunion households. Therefore, to get a sense of the challenge that the forgotten majority poses to the Democrats, in particular, we find it useful to isolate the group—nonunion forgotten majority voters—in which electoral improvement is most necessary.

We further break down forgotten majority voters outside of unions by gender to get a sense of where the challenges are most acute within this group. Finally, we divide minority voters not in unions by race—blacks, Hispanics, and Asians/other minorities—thus reflecting their large observed differences in voting behavior. This produces eight basic groups of voters, together comprising the whole electorate. Union household members are in one category; and then, all limited to nonunion households, we have blacks, Hispanics, and Asians/other minorities; and, for whites, men and women, split between college-educated and forgotten majority.[3]

The Democratic Challenge

The Democrats are strong in three of these categories: union households and (nonunion) blacks and Hispanics. For example, in 1998, Democrats received 64 percent of the vote in union households,[4] 89 percent of the vote among nonunion blacks, and 61 percent of the nonunion Hispanic vote. This Democratic-leaning base is about a third of the electorate, with union household members comprising about 22 percent[5] of voters in 1996, and nonunion blacks and Hispanics another 11 percent (see Table 5.1).

TABLE 5.1   Building Blocks of the Next Majority

		Democratic Support		
Group	Percent of Voters[1]	1996 House Support[2]	1998 House Support	1996 Presidential Support
Union Households	22%	63%	64%	59%
Not in Union Households:				
Blacks	8	80	89	83
Hispanics	3	69	61	72
Asian/Other Minorities	1	52	55	46
Forgotten Majority	45	44	39	41
Men	19	40	35	33
Women	26	48	42	46
College-Educated Whites	21	36	40	39
Men	11	32	36	31
Women	11	41	44	48

[1] Based on 1996 data.

[2] Based on two-party vote.

Source: Authors' analysis of 1996 and 1998 VNS exit polls and 1996 Census Voter Supplement data.

For many, strong Democratic support among such voters suggests a natural road to Democratic dominance that would avoid the thorny problem of the forgotten majority: Expand the Democratic base either through increased turnout amoung these base groups (e.g., higher black turnout) or through these groups themselves becoming larger (e.g., more Hispanics in the population). At least in the short term, however, this strategy has only limited potential.

Members of Union Households?

Take union household voters. The obvious way for the Democrats to reach more of these voters is to increase the turnout rates of current union household members. The problem with this strategy is that these voters already turn out at high rates. Union household turnout in 1998, for example, was 53 percent,[6] compared to

40 percent among the voting-age population as a whole and just 37 percent for nonunion voters. And even after controlling for education, income, race, and other characteristics, there's still a substantial union effect on participation: Union household members, all else being equal, simply participate more.

But while the fact that union household members vote heavily, and tend to vote Democratic, is good news for the Democratic party, it also suggests some limits to just how much more water the party can get from this particular stone. Could union household participation be driven to 75 or 85 percent? It's possible, but pretty unlikely, as it means that such voters would have to increase their already-high turnout rates by another 20 to 25 percentage points, a very tough proposition indeed. This is not to say that union turnout rates can't be bumped up in particular elections[7] or, especially if the election is a close one, that they can't play a very important role. But it seems very unlikely that dramatically *increased* union turnout will play more than a minor role in building a lasting Democratic majority coalition.

Then again, Democrats might try to increase the number of people in union households by making it easier for workers to join unions. Historically, the real change over time in the political role of union voters has been driven not by declining Democratic support rates or declining turnout rates, but by the declining relative weight of unions in the workforce and, therefore, by their declining weight in American society as a whole. Turning this trend in the other direction would be a considerable boon to the Democrats. For example, the percentage of the workforce that was unionized in 1960 was at least 9 percentage points higher than it is today,[8] and the share of union household members among voters was, in rough correspondence, about 7 points higher.[9] At current rates of partisan loyalty, making up that post-1960 decline in union household voters would produce a corresponding increase in the average Democratic vote of around 1 percentage point, both in the Congressional and presidential vote. If we assume that what the Democrats need is to raise their average percentage of the vote from current levels (49–50 percent) to a "normal" level of perhaps 53 percent,[10] such an increment makes a substantial contribution to getting them there.

Easier said than done, however. Given the very modest progress of even the new leaders of the AFL-CIO in increasing union density (so far, they have managed only to slow the *decline* in unionization), a blueprint for a new Democratic majority should not count on much beyond the current base of union household voters to work with—though maintaining that base, of course, is critical. In the end, it is certainly possible that increased organizing efforts may yield a significant dividend of increased unionization and, consequently, increased union voters. But a serious Democratic strategy that effectively circumvents the forgotten majority must be based on reaching the current electorate, not a projected future one.

Blacks Not in Union Households?

Black voters offer a similarly limited resource for the Democrats. Their staunch support for the Democratic party is one of the great, undisputed political facts of our time. Election after election, for offices high and low, black voters overwhelmingly support Democrats by 80 to 90 percent or more. Given these support levels, it's close to pure electoral gold for the Democrats to increase the black vote. But how possible would this be on a regular basis?

A perennial source of Democratic hope, black turnout is just as perennially misunderstood. After the 1996 presidential election, for example, some argued that black *male* turnout had taken a huge jump—underscoring the possibilities of a base expansion strategy.[11] But it turned out that these data, based on exit polls, were contradicted by more reliable Census Voter Supplement data showing that black men actually exhibited a *decline* in turnout (of 4 points, a bit more than the 3-point decline among black women).[12] And the voting share of black men remained about the same: 4 percent of the active electorate.

Similarly, 1998 was generally considered to be an exceptionally good year for black turnout, as blacks turned out to oppose the Republican Congress and in support of President Clinton. But the overall increase in black turnout was only about 3 percentage points over 1994; and the increase in black representation among voters, about half that.[13] That was still an impressive performance in a year when overall turnout went down, but it illustrates just how difficult it is to produce a large overall increase in black turnout, even in a favorable situation where get-out-the-vote efforts are deemed successful. (Large increases in particular state or local races are a different issue.)

Part of the reason for this difficulty is that blacks are no longer as underrepresented as they used to be among voters, and it is hence more difficult to produce large increases in turnout; in short, the easiest voters to get to the polls are already there. Consistent with this analysis the turnout rate of blacks in 1998 was only 2 percentage points lower than the turnout rate of the population as a whole. This difference was small enough that, even given the somewhat lower turnout rate, the representation of blacks among voters and among the age-eligible electorate was roughly equal: about 11 percent in each case. Indeed, if other demographics (education, income, etc.) are controlled for, data from this and other elections show that blacks are, at this point, more likely, not less likely, to turn out than whites.

And so with nonunion blacks, as with union household members, it's not plausible to think that their participation rates could be increased dramatically. In addition, blacks remain a relatively small part of the U.S. electorate—just over one-tenth—so the impact of whatever turnout increases can be generated will be further limited.[14] Blacks are clearly a central part of the Democratic base, and it's essential that the Democrats retain them. But they cannot function as a substitute for the forgotten majority in the Democrats' quest for a new coalition.

Hispanics Not in Union Households?

While the support of Hispanics for Democrats has been considerably less staunch than that of blacks, and in some areas (e.g., Florida) is in fact quite weak, overall support levels of Hispanics for Democrats are still quite high—in the 60 to 70 percent range. Given these support levels, expanding Hispanic representation among active voters would presumably be a clear boon to the Democrats. But, here again we've got questions about how much and how fast current levels of participation can be increased, as well as about the magnitude of the associated effect.

An optimistic answer to the first part of this question was suggested by reports of dramatically increased Hispanic turnout in the 1996 election. According to widely cited data from exit polls, Hispanic representation among voters almost doubled (from 2.3 percent in 1992 to 4.5 percent in 1996). This implied a strong increase in Hispanic turnout of 7 percentage points (in an election where overall turnout went *down* 6 points) and an increase among Hispanics of almost 2 million votes. But again, the more reliable Census data suggest that the amount of change in the Hispanic vote was much less dramatic. Indeed, as with black turnout, the Census data say that Hispanic turnout actually went *down* by a couple of percentage points.

Given that Hispanics' proportion of the population increased between 1992 and 1996 and Hispanic turnout went down *less* than that of the rest of the population in an abysmally low turnout year, they still increased their share of the electorate—albeit more modestly than exit polls suggested—from just under 4 to just under 5 percent (an increase of about 700,000 votes[15]).

The 1998 Census data tell essentially the same story. Despite reports of a huge surge in the Hispanic vote, again usually based on exit poll findings, the Census data indicate modest increases of about 1 percentage point compared to 1994, both in Hispanic turnout and in the Hispanic share of active voters.

In the long run though, Hispanics' growing share of the population *will* substantially increase their share of the active electorate. According to Census projections,[16] the Hispanic share of the voting-age population should grow more than 50 percent over the next two decades—rising from a little under 10 percent to about 15 percent by the year 2020.[17] As a very rough estimate, this growth might increase the Hispanic proportion of the voting electorate to about 8 percent.[18] And at present rates of partisan support (as with our presumptive restoration of unions to their 1960s levels, but with a lot more confidence in the growth of the underlying base), this larger proportion might increase the average Democratic share of the vote about 1 percentage point. Again, such an increase would be significant in the context of developing a normal national Democratic vote of around 53 percent and, given the regional concentration of Hispanics, would have larger effects in several Southwestern and Western states.[19]

But these are long-run changes. In the short run, the basic racial structure of the voting electorate is going to change only slowly. As with union members and blacks, then, so with Hispanics. A successful Democratic coalition-building strategy needs to keep Hispanics as part of the base, but they do not provide a plausible substitute for increased support among the forgotten majority.

Back to the Forgotten Majority

So, expansion of the Democrats' existing base, at least anytime soon, doesn't seem to pave the road to a new Democratic majority. The current Democratic coalition, which most emphatically is *not* a majority, is already doing a fair job of getting these base voters to the polls. It could always do better, of course; but even if it did, there are arithmetical limits to the likely effect.

So, what would pave that road? Inescapably, the forgotten majority. Forgotten majority voters, even excluding those in unions where the Democrats do relatively well, make up close to half the electorate (45 percent) and are now voting Democratic for the House at only a 39–44(1998/1996) percent rate, and for president (1996) at a 41 percent rate (again, see Table 5.1). Just as Republicans made great gains in the 1970s and 1980s by, as Richard Nixon liked to put it, "hunting where the ducks are" (in that case, within the expanding ranks of disaffected whites, particularly in the South), so the Democrats have to go after the biggest pond of ducks—the unorganized ranks of the new white working class. In fact, they don't even need a majority of such voters. Just breaking even would bring both their House and presidential share of the two-party vote to 53 percent. Obviously adequate for the presidency, this level of support would also, almost certainly, be enough to take back the House and would bring popular support for House Democrats back to pre-1994 levels. (Recall that the Democrats averaged 53 percent of the two-party vote throughout the 1980s and early 1990s.)

Considering this target group by sex, we find that forgotten majority men are clearly the tougher nut. Almost one-fifth of the electorate (19 percent) of the voting electorate, they're now voting Democratic at only a 35 percent rate for the House (1998) and an even more anemic 33 percent rate for the presidency. They would thus have to be moved 15 and 17 points, respectively, for the Democrats simply to break even.

Forgotten majority women in this group present a somewhat easier target for the Democrats. A larger share of the active electorate than their male counterparts—a quarter, as against a fifth—they are substantially more supportive of Democrats, with

42 percent now supporting them for the House (1998) and 46 percent for the presidency. The Democrats could thus break even with this group by increasing their support a comparatively modest 8 and 4 points, respectively.

But as promising as the forgotten majority women's vote is, getting to parity with the Republicans among the new white working class is still going to require some serious mobilization among unorganized forgotten majority men. For example, even if support among forgotten majority women in this group increased to more than 50 percent, Democrats would still need to raise support to, say, the mid-40s among their male counterparts (a not insubstantial 10-point rise) for an even split overall among these voters to even begin to be feasible.

This might seem a daunting task, but keep in mind that House Democrats regularly attained these levels of support among forgotten majority voters, including men, until the early 1990s. So we are not talking about an outcome without precedent. Furthermore, the Democrats simply have no choice; they cannot construct a reliable majority without these voters.

But what if going after the forgotten majority alienates the Democratic base? It is certainly possible that some trade-offs in support may be involved. But again, the Democrats have little choice but to risk such trade-offs, while seeking to minimize them; otherwise, they will condemn themselves to, at best, a perpetual stalemate with the Republicans. Besides, as we shall see in the next section, the best approach to mobilizing the forgotten majority lies in universalist, transracial issues that should have substantial appeal to the Democratic base as well. If so, the trade-offs in support for the Democrats could be minimal to nonexistent.

Another objection—and this applies only to the presidential level—might be that third-party competition means the Democrats can get by without improving their performance among the forgotten majority. This is a dangerous line of analysis for the

Democrats, in that it presupposes a fairly successful third-party effort. But there is no guarantee this will be so, even in the short run. Reform party candidacies in upcoming elections could easily implode and generate negligible electoral support, leaving a Democratic presidential candidate who was relying on third-party competition unprepared to meet the challenge of improving forgotten majority support.

Furthermore, even with a serious Reform party showing, presidential Democrats can get by only in the narrow and short-run sense of mustering a sufficient plurality to edge their Republican opponents. Even if they are able to do so, they will still lack the popular support necessary to break the partisan stalemate and policy paralysis in Washington and forge a new majority governing coalition. Therefore, presidential Democrats, just like Congressional Democrats, will eventually need to capture a solid majority of the popular vote, and the only way to do that is through substantially increased support among unorganized sectors of the new white working class.

A final objection is that the Democrats may be able to wait out the forgotten majority, as inexorable demographic trends attenuate their political influence. It could be a long wait. Extrapolating from current educational attainment trends and Bureau of the Census population projections, the forgotten majority might dip under 50 percent of voters by the year 2020. That's two decades from now and even then, we estimate they'll still comprise 48 percent of voters—a huge group that would be difficult, if not impossible, for the Democrats to work around.

A New Base Among the Learning Class?

Put the arithmetic another way. If Democrats aren't able to appeal effectively to the forgotten majority, and expansion of their current base is not sufficient, they will have to rely on increasing their support among college-educated whites. Indeed, to listen to some orthodox New Democrats, this appears to be the party's major goal. They argue that since "the New Economy favors a rising Learning Class over a declining working class" (see the quote at the beginning of Chapter 2), and since there is an "educational bias in the electorate" that favors the college-educated, the party must focus on highly educated voters.[20] Not counting black and Hispanic college-educated voters, who already vote Democratic at extremely high rates, we are left with college-educated whites. What should be said here is simply this: It won't work.

College-educated white voters are, of course, substantially more affluent than their working-class counterparts and consequently tend to have lower levels of concern about economic problems and less inclination toward activist approaches to those problems. Moreover, once the very small, unionized, Democratic-leaning component is separated out, this group comprises just over one-fifth of the electorate—less than half the size of their working-class counterparts—and voted Democratic for the House at only a 36 percent (1996) to 40 percent (1998) rate and for president at a 39 percent rate.

This group is divided about equally between men and women. Once again, the men are substantially more conservative. Only 31 percent voted Democratic in the presidential election of 1996, and only 36 percent voted Democratic in the House election of 1998. Moreover, other public opinion data show that this group has strongly conservative views on everything from budget and taxes to education, trade, and health care—far more so than either working-class white men or college-educated white women. This fact makes them unlikely candidates for Democratic conversion.

The Democrats are doing substantially better with college-educated white women not in unions. About 44 percent supported the Democrats for the House in 1998, and an impressive 48 percent supported Clinton for president in 1996. These relatively strong figures have fueled Democrats' belief that they should target college-educated voters, particularly women, rather than working-class men.

This suggestion is a bad one for two reasons. One is size: The number of unorganized forgotten majority men is nearly twice that of unorganized college-educated white women. Hence, to make the same contribution to raising the Democratic vote as simply breaking even among these forgotten majority men, the Democrats would have to capture over 65 percent of these college-educated women for the House and over 75 percent(!) of them for president. This seems beyond the bounds of plausibility.

The second reason is that the relatively high Democratic support rate of this group is overwhelmingly driven by highly educated women who have received a postgraduate education (law school, medical school, or graduate school). These women voted 53 percent Democratic for the House in 1998 and 56 percent Democratic for president in 1996. Those in this group with just a four-year college degree were much more conservative, supporting Democrats at rates of only 40 percent and 43 percent, respectively. But this four-year-degree group is more numerous; the postgraduate women group amount to only about 3 percent of voters. This ratio makes it doubly implausible to focus on these college-educated white women, since the liberal component of the group is so small.

Of course, the Democrats could focus on both the forgotten majority and college-educated, particularly postgraduate, white women. There is nothing intrinsically wrong with this solution, given adequate resources. But the essential point here is that the latter cannot substitute for the former. If the Democrats can improve their performance with the forgotten majority, additional support from postgraduate white women is icing on the cake. But without the forgotten majority voters, there is no cake to be iced.

Will the Real Suburban Voter Please Stand Up?

The above analysis sketches the basic demographic contours of the Democrats' challenge as they seek to forge a new majority. It reflects the forgotten majority's dominance of the voting electorate and suggests strongly that the Democrats can forge that majority only from swing voters who look quite different from the archetypal suburban swing voters beloved by commentators and political consultants. Those suburban swing voters, the latest version of whom were the "soccer moms" of the 1996 election, are usually envisioned as having high household incomes, college educations, and so on—as being Volvo-drivers, if you will, rather than the Cavalier-drivers we've been describing.

But our analysis has been based on national data. Could it be that suburban swing voters are mostly Volvo-drivers, instead of Cavalier-drivers, as national swing voters are? Not according to our analysis of Bureau of the Census and exit poll data. The percentage of forgotten majority voters in the suburbs is pretty much identical to their percentage in the country as a whole—about 55 percent (and far higher than the percentage of college-educated whites). Furthermore, forgotten majority voters in the suburbs—overall and broken down by gender—*vote* the same way as forgotten majority voters in the country as a whole. Finally, forgotten majority voters in the suburbs are the "suburban swing" in the literal sense that they are the suburban voters who swung the most from election to election in the 1990s. That is, across the board, working-class and low- to moderate-income whites in the suburbs have been far more volatile than their college-educated and affluent counterparts.

So, from virtually every standpoint, the Democrats' target voters in the suburbs are precisely the ones we identified earlier in our national analysis: forgotten majority voters, especially those not in union households. Only if they succeed in capturing the loyalty of far more of these voters will they stand a chance of forging a dominant majority, both in the suburbs and across the nation as a whole.

The Republican Challenge

We have seen that the Democrats must appeal to the forgotten majority. But what of the Republicans? They start with the following strengths and weaknesses, which are basically a mirror image of the Democrats: They do very poorly among union household voters, and among nonunion blacks and Hispanics; they do relatively well among both unorganized forgotten majority voters and their richer, college-educated counterparts. And, throughout, they do especially well among men. The two basic options for Republicans are to cut into the Democratic base among union households and minorities, or to increase their support among whites not in unions, particularly women.

Cracking the Democratic Base

Can the Republicans crack the core Democratic base among union household members and minorities? Possibly, but only with great difficulty. The most inviting arithmetic target, given its size, is the block of union household voters. Politically, however, we don't see it happening. At least at the level of federal politics, unions are now better organized than they've been in some time, and they are more resolutely Democratic than ever. Indeed, the last two elections have been disastrous for the Republicans among union household voters; they polled only 33 percent (1996) to 36 percent (1998) for the House and a miserable 28 percent for president in 1996. This block has been effectively organized for the Democrats, and we think it will be hard to break.

Blacks not in unions seem an even less likely target. They have shown no signs whatsoever of straying from the Democratic fold in recent elections, so Republican efforts in this direction would, in all likelihood, be wasted. The GOP should probably announce that it's not racist, and announce that again and again and again. But the play to black voters is difficult. After all, these voters have memories spread across several decades of Republican indifference, if not hostility, to their concerns.

Perhaps the best bet for breaking into the Democratic base lies in the burgeoning Hispanic voter group. In the 1998 election, Hispanics not in unions voted 39 percent Republican for the House. In some state elections, such as the Texas gubernatorial election, Republican support levels were much higher. While it would be a mistake to read such signs as a harbinger of massive defections from the Democratic camp, they do suggest an openness among the rapidly changing and diverse Hispanic population to Republican appeals.

This openness is worth pursuing, to be sure; but the fact remains that the electoral weight of Hispanics will remain relatively small for many years (see our earlier discussion of Hispanic population projections). Therefore, the potential contribution of this group to a new national-level Republican majority, even under the best of circumstances, will remain small (though on the state level, it could be important in several Southwestern states and in California).

Reaching Out to Forgotten Majority Women

A strategy of breaking into the Democrats' base, therefore, seems most unpromising for the Republicans—at least as a primary focus. Instead, they have to make most of their progress by building on their strengths among whites outside of unions.

The first move along such lines is to bring their presidential support levels among this group up to their Congressional support levels. If they don't, there is no chance for a new Republican majority. However, even if they do, such success will not, by itself, be sufficient to produce that majority. They will need to improve their performance among nonunion white voters over their current Congressional levels, which are only enough to put them at rough parity with the Democrats (the House vote was close to evenly split in both the 1996 and 1998 elections), but not enough for a dominant coalition.

The most effective way for them to do this is to improve their performance among nonunion white women. In the 1998 election, for example, Republicans already received roughly 65 percent of the vote from nonunion white men. It is probably not realistic for them to push those support levels up much higher—though maintaining that support is key, especially among forgotten majority men, who overall provided about 30 percent of Republican votes in the 1998 election. Among women, however, where support levels were 7 to 9 points lower, increased support is more realistic. The key group here is *unorganized forgotten majority women*. If their Republican support levels can simply be brought in line with those of their male counterparts, that outcome in and of itself would be enough to give the Republicans their new majority. In comparison, to have the same effect, Republicans would have to receive 75 percent support among college-educated white women outside of unions. Especially given the Democratic leanings of the most highly educated part of this group, women with a postgraduate education, this seems highly unlikely.

The Inescapable Problem

The political arithmetic of the American electorate is unforgiving. Whether either major party likes it or not—to say nothing of any third party—the road to the next successful political coalition runs straight through the forgotten majority. The Democrats have to reach toward the break-even point among these voters, especially by strengthening their performance among men (while continuing to turn out their current base). The Republicans have to intensify their dominance of forgotten majority voters, especially by enhancing their performance among women (or break into the Democrats' base). For both parties, these are daunting challenges with no obvious or risk-free solutions.

But, given a willingness to face these electoral facts and take direct aim at mobilizing the forgotten majority, we believe either party could reach its electoral targets and, in the process, realign American politics. In the next chapter, we consider how the mobilization of the forgotten majority might actually be accomplished.

SIX

Mobilizing the Forgotten Majority

[E]ven as the U.S. economy exits the millennium with an unprecedented bang, there are signs of unease. . . . It's the puzzling anomaly of the New Economy. In the greatest period of wealth creation in U.S. history, the average American, it seems, is living in another era. "In the real world, people are still living from paycheck to paycheck," says Princeton University economist Henry Farber. "The tremendous wealth creation has by and large gone to the people at the top." . . . [M]any Americans are torn over the benefits of the New Economy and globalization . . . 75% of those surveyed say the benefits of the New Economy have been distributed unevenly.

— *Business Week*, DECEMBER 27, 1999[1]

So, FROM EITHER PARTY'S PERSPECTIVE, the problem—mobilizing the forgotten majority—is clear enough; the solution, less so. This is a challenge not just for the parties but for our country. As we enter the 21st century, we stand on the verge, finally, of a truly inclusive national greatness. But to meet this challenge, we need a new era of strong government—one in which government doesn't sit on the sidelines but makes a serious effort to solve the great national problems that divide Americans from one another. That new era depends on the mobilization of the forgotten majority. In the absence of that mobilization, the future role of government seems likely to be limited and the country will be the poorer for it.

What Does the Forgotten Majority Want?

The first step in figuring out how to mobilize these voters is understanding what they want. To do so, we need to review where the 1990s left them, both economically and politically.

The New Economy

The late 1990s, especially from 1997 on, were very good years for the U.S. economy in general and the forgotten majority in particular. As we outlined in Chapter 2, rapidly rising wages and incomes accompanied strong growth, low inflation, and low unemployment. The forgotten majority shared fully in the economic benefits of this robust performance and, as a result, has become relatively optimistic about economic conditions.

People have also become guardedly optimistic about the future potential of the new economy. They see many positive opportunities that are provided by the processes of technological change and globalization and believe that these processes are irreversible anyway.[2] The big question for most is how to find their place in the new economy, given the tremendous changes that are taking place. As we saw in Chapter 2, Americans continue to believe that hard work is the key to achieving the American Dream. They're just not sure how to make that work in the new economy.

The strong economic performance and apparent potential of the new economy, along with political developments in the 1990s, have done much to soften the pragmatic conservatism of the forgotten majority. A society in which hard work is, at least in the short term, being properly rewarded—and might possibly be rewarded even more in the future—is a society whose values are getting back in synch and where government may not be quite the problem the forgotten majority once thought it was.

Of course, this is not to say the problems of the forgotten majority have disappeared. As stated in the quote at the beginning of the chapter, people are still living from paycheck to paycheck, even if those paychecks have grown bigger and they can now afford some things they couldn't before. Two decades of stagnant or declining wages, after all, will take considerably more time to overcome. The Great Divide between the college-educated and the non-college-educated remains; in fact, it is as wide as ever. And members of the forgotten majority have an abundance of long-term worries: about earning enough money to lead the kind of life they want, about the impact of globalization, about not having enough money for retirement, about being unable to save enough money to put a child through college, about being unable to afford necessary health care when a family member gets sick.[3] We call these and related worries the "New Insecurity," reflecting economic problems that the new economy has, as yet, done little to solve.

The New Insecurity

The forgotten majority, of course, is fully affected by the entire range of New Insecurity problems and, in every instance, much more so than its college-educated counterparts. In addition, where polling data permit appropriate breakdowns, levels of concern about New Insecurity problems are stronger among the forgotten majority than among the population as a whole.

These New Insecurity issues start with health care. About 44 million Americans now lack health insurance, and their numbers continue to grow every year. In addition, HMOs now dominate the health-care marketplace, a development the public is convinced has reduced the quality of health care. Finally, Americans worry tremendously about medical-care costs and are overwhelmingly convinced that these costs are getting worse.[4] The new economy, whatever its other virtues, does not offer much of a solution to this problem.

Another key problem is retirement security. More than half of all private-sector workers do not have access to a pension plan through their employer; and, as noted in Chapter 2, those that do are increasingly likely to have to fund that pension themselves, through a "defined contribution" 401(k)-type plan, rather than to receive a guaranteed pension on their retirement ("defined benefit"), as was generally the case twenty-five years ago. Nor does it seem likely that increased ownership of stocks will solve the retirement security problem: 57 percent of American households do not own a single share of stock, either within or outside a pension plan, and only one-third own stock valued at more that $5,000. No wonder 78 percent of Americans say, even in the middle of an economic boom, that they are concerned about not having enough money for retirement.[5] The new economy, with its emphasis on job shifting and flexible work arrangements, seems ill-suited to filling in these holes and so far has not done so.

Then there are the related issues of education and training. The new economy is defined as much as anything else by an emphasis on education and skills. The public endorses this idea and tends to believe that those who get the proper education and skills will prosper—and those who don't, won't.[6] But how can people be sure that their children are getting a good education and will be able to acquire the right skills? For that matter, how can they be sure that their own skills are adequate in this rapidly shifting economic world? And, if these skills become inadequate, how can they be sure they'll be able to upgrade them in an effective and timely manner? Thus, as the new economy holds out the promise of a more prosperous and highly skilled society, it simultaneously creates a high-stakes problem for most that it cannot do much, on its own, to solve.

Fueling the concern about access to skills training is another problem: job security. Part of the conventional description of the new economy is the idea that workers are no longer tied to specific companies—or "lifetime jobs"—and tend to shift positions frequently in response to changing opportunities. When voluntary, such job changing has a benign face, but when involuntary it is an aspect of the New Insecurity. Survey data suggest that workers in the 1990s, despite the strength of the economy, are increasingly worried that they cannot count on job security, even if they do a good job.[7] And once they lose a job involuntarily, workers suffer an average 14 percent wage loss. About 29 percent of them also lose their health benefits, if they had them on the job they lost.[8]

Another part of the New Insecurity, and very much related to the problem of job security, is the impact of globalization, an issue forcefully raised by the late-1999 protests in Seattle against the World Trade Organization (WTO). Americans tend to see globalization as an economic process with great potential, but one that, so far, has had negative effects on American workers and their jobs. They are further convinced that globalization today is primarily benefiting business and that trade policy making is driven by business interests. And they are concerned that, without appropriate labor and environmental standards, the effects on American workers will continue to be negative, if not actually worsen.[9] Thus, as the new economy becomes increasingly global, it simultaneously creates a problem that more globalization, by itself, cannot address.

Another problem that good economic performance has not solved is the rise of work-family pressures and conflicts. Indeed, many workers are taking advantage of the tight labor market to make more money by putting in more hours, which simply intensifies pressures on the family. And, of course, children not attending—or after attending—school need care when parents are working all these hours, posing a difficult and high-stakes challenge to most families. Survey data confirm that parents feel these time pressures acutely, believe they are getting worse, and find the struggle to secure affordable, high-quality child care very to extremely difficult.[10] It is hard to see how the new economy, even if the current expansion continues, will do much to alleviate these insecurities.

Finally, the very success and strength of the economy in the last several years create its own insecurity. People have now become used to a very tight labor market, with rising wages and incomes, not to mention soaring stock portfolios for those who have them. In fact, they have taken advantage of this good economic news to go on a spending spree. The personal savings rate has reached and even dipped below zero, while levels of consumer debt have reached record highs.[11] This means that if the economy turns down, there will not only be less money for households to spend but also little savings to draw on and considerable debt to be paid. Such vulnerability adds considerably to the financial and psychological stake people have in continued fast economic growth.

The New Austerity

As the new economy has developed, and left the New Insecurity in its wake, there is another key element of the political-economic landscape that must be mentioned. This is the evolution of the "New Austerity," a fiscal politics that puts huge constraints on the ability of either party to launch new initiatives. Under the New Austerity, America's budget surplus has been fetishized into something that must be maintained at all costs,[12] regardless of whether—and how much—it is truly responsible for today's prosperity[13] and regardless of how many social needs must go begging in the meantime.

Let's review how this fiscal politics has evolved. It all started with the 1993 budget deal, which made substantial progress in reducing the budget deficit and also enshrined deficit reduction as the overriding priority of fiscal politics. This was followed by Clinton's commitment, in June 1995, to actually balancing the budget. These fiscal constraints already made it quite difficult to argue for new initiatives that might require large expenditures.

The 1997 budget deal marked a radical ratcheting-up of fiscal constraints, despite, paradoxically, the beginnings of fiscal plenty. In order to produce a future balanced budget, the deal mandated unrealistically low levels of domestic spending (the "budget caps") that would result in future real cuts in already-existing programs but left no fiscal room for new ones. Then, when projected budget surpluses started appearing way ahead of schedule in late 1997, the Clinton administration, by pledging to "save Social Security first" in effect took these surpluses off the table. This ensured that the surpluses couldn't be used for tax cuts, as the Republicans wanted, but also that they couldn't be used for new spending. Instead, the surpluses were allocated to paying down the national debt, ostensibly until such time as the retirement system's long-term solvency problems were solved.

The final act in the development of today's fiscal politics was the acceptance by the Democrats of the Republicans' "Social Security lockbox" concept. Under the lockbox approach, the part of the projected budget surplus attributable to Social Security— that is, to the excess of incoming Social Security taxes over outgoing Social Security benefits—is walled off from the rest of the budget and deemed untouchable. What this means concretely is that the Social Security surplus, which is almost three-quarters of the entire budget surplus, is used to pay down the national debt, rather than to fund the activities of government—as it had been used for decades—or to provide a tax cut. As most economists acknowledge, allocating the Social Security surplus in this way does nothing directly to ensure the long-term health of the Social Security system,[14] its stated purpose, and probably has only modestly positive effects on the economy as a whole.[15]

But whatever its effects on the Social Security system and the economy, the lockbox incontrovertibly puts fiscal politics in a straitjacket. Instead of almost $3 trillion in surplus funds to spend over ten years, an average of $300 billion a year, the lockbox leaves about $750 billion over ten years, an average of only $75 billion a year, on the table. This is an enormous difference that severely limits the scale of domestic initiatives that can be undertaken, despite the fiscal plenty and the booming economy. The paradoxical nature of these fiscal politics has been well noted by economic columnist Matthew Miller, who observed: "[T]he center of political gravity has shifted so spectacularly [since 1992] that the bold investment agenda for lifelong learning, research and development, and infrastructure that was a winner in an era of scarcity can't even be discussed by a Democratic administration when it could at last be funded."[16] "Putting people first" is out; the New Austerity reigns triumphant.

But the New Austerity presents a big problem for both parties. To the extent that either wishes to address the New Insecurity and the forgotten majority voters for whom these problems are very real, there is relatively little to offer them other than modifying already-existing programs and providing some very modest new initiatives, given these fiscal constraints. This contradiction will only deepen if and when the economy enters a downturn and families have to curtail their free-spending ways, pay their debts, and worry even more about job and health insurance loss. At that point, there will be a ratcheting-up of demand for action to address the New Insecurity, but government—of whatever party—will find it difficult to provide such action unless it breaks the fiscal consensus.

Reuniting the Values of the Forgotten Majority with Its Economic Experience

What would it actually take to address the New Insecurity in a way that could mobilize forgotten majority voters? In our view, the key is reuniting the core values of the forgotten majority with its economic experience. Consider the following possibilities.

- *If a criminal has a right to a lawyer, you have a right to a doctor.* This is a great line from Harris Wofford's successful Senate campaign of 1991, and it sounds just the right note for the forgotten majority. If a criminal has a right to a lawyer, hard-working, law-abiding citizens should be provided with access to health care. They should not be left out in the cold just because they're unlucky enough to lose their job or to work for a company that doesn't provide affordable health insurance.
- *People who work hard all their lives should have an adequate income in their retirement.* Those people who have been willing to work hard for decades and support their families should not find, upon their retirement, that they hardly have enough money to live on. It is not fair to punish people who work for employers that don't provide pensions or who have made too little money to save much for their retirement.
- *Americans have a right to the best education their tax money can buy.* In this rapidly changing economy, American workers and their children must have access to appropriate education—elementary, secondary, college, and beyond. Otherwise, even if they work hard, they'll fall behind eco-

nomically. And that's not right. Whatever it takes, the money should be provided to make sure that doesn't happen.

- *Those willing to work hard should be able to get the training they want to get the job they need.* One aspect of the new economy is that people frequently have to or want to change jobs. But they should not be penalized because they can't get access to training they would be perfectly willing and able to go through. That's just not fair.

- *In today's global economy, we all have the right to a decent wage and to speak our minds and organize.* American workers shouldn't be competing with workers in other countries whose wages are artificially depressed by the absence of even minimal standards and democratic freedoms. That's not fair to workers abroad or to workers at home.

- *People who work hard should also be able to spend enough time with their families.* Hard work shouldn't destroy family life and parents' relationships with their children. That's not the American Dream. We have to find ways to give workers more time to spend as parents, instead of the other way around.

- *Women who work outside the home should have access to affordable, quality child care.* Those women who want, or need, to work in today's society should not have to sacrifice the welfare of their children to do so. They and their children have a right to affordable, quality child care.

- *We should make whatever investments are necessary to keep the economy growing fast in the future.* Fast economic growth benefits all Americans who are willing to work. It's a good use of tax money to spend whatever is necessary to keep the economy going.

This approach builds on the core values of the forgotten majority—opportunity, fair reward for effort, the centrality of hard work and achievement, and social commitment. By no means would it make everybody in the forgotten majority rich. But it would give them all a fair shot at a dignified, reasonably prosperous and secure life—in short, a middle-class life as it once was understood. We believe such a prospect would be enormously appealing to forgotten majority voters.

Of course, Republicans and Democrats would have very different ideas about how to implement this approach. But implement it they must if they are serious about mobilizing these voters and building a new majority. The New Insecurity, as we have argued, will not be eliminated by the natural workings of the new economy, so the need to confront it in a politically viable way is inescapable. The sooner the parties acknowledge this fact, and the associated need to discard or substantially modify the New Austerity, the sooner they will reap the consequent electoral rewards—or lose them to the other party.

The Universalism of the Forgotten Majority Approach

An important aspect of the approach we have outlined is its universalism. As pointed out earlier, the values that underlie this approach are not confined to the forgotten majority but, rather, are widely shared across lines of class and race. And the principles it seeks to establish in the areas of health, retirement, education, and so on also have universalist appeal. This is especially true with respect to the problems and concerns of working-class blacks and Hispanics, who make up the overwhelming majority of these populations. There is nothing in the program outlined above that would not appeal to these voters, even as it serves to mobilize the forgotten majority. In fact, given that the New Insecurity probably affects working-class blacks and Hispanics more than any other part of the population, we would expect them to be particularly receptive to the approach sketched here.

A Democratic Approach

The parties would each have very different ways of crafting their appeal to the forgotten majority, even if they accepted the basic approach we have outlined. They would also confront very different challenges as they attempted to do so. Here's how we believe the Democrats might be successful in crafting such an appeal and how, in the process, they might overcome their long-standing problems with the forgotten majority.

The essence of a successful Democratic approach would be large, concrete improvements in institutionalizing the principles outlined in the previous section. That doesn't mean achieving them entirely in the short run, but it does mean substantial progress, so that the forgotten majority can actually see their economic experience realigning with their values through government action. Following are some examples of what we mean, focusing on recently important voter concerns.

Start with health care. Defending Medicare is not enough, since this program is intended only for those sixty-five and over and, by definition, constitutes not progress but "holding the line." A better way to move forward is to guarantee health coverage for children. This is a particularly popular goal, and an eminently attainable one; it is also relatively inexpensive[17] because children are, on average, a very healthy group. But, as recent experience attests, piecemeal approaches do not work: The number of children without health insurance is now about 11 million despite the current federal subsidy program run through the states, and a strong case can be made that only a government guarantee of such coverage—"Medicare for kids," basically—is likely to do the job.[18]

Of course, as the majority of uninsured are not children, "Medicare for kids" would leave a lot of people uncovered. However, the logic of "If a criminal has a right to a lawyer, your kids

have a right to a doctor" leads straight to the principle "If a criminal has a right to a lawyer, your entire family has a right to a doctor." So guaranteeing health coverage for children is a giant step
toward establishing this principle even if it falls short of fully
achieving it.

Or take the issue of retirement security. Again, defending Social Security is not enough. That would merely preserve an inadequate status quo, since most people will need more than their
Social Security benefits to ensure a secure retirement. A better
way forward is to guarantee every worker a tax-sheltered, supple-
mental 401(k)-type savings account outside of Social Security, administered by the government and including federal
contributions and matching funds for low- to middle-income
workers. This does not quite get us to "People who work hard all
their lives should have an adequate income in their retirement,"
but it gets us closer and clearly helps establish the principle.

Another key issue is education. By and large, the forgotten majority is dissatisfied with America's educational system, so defending existing programs and funding levels won't do. Instead,
the Democrats might focus on filling obvious gaps in the system.
One obvious gap is limited access to education outside of the
standard K–12 school day and school year. Democrats could
therefore advocate (1) providing universal access to preschool,
including full funding for Head Start; (2) keeping schools open
twelve hours a day, twelve months a year (the "12/12 schedule"),
with enrichment and remedial educational activities available at
times when regular classes are not meeting (e.g., before and
after school hours, and during breaks); and (3) creating a college loan program[19] whereby students' repayments depend on
their actual earnings after they leave school. These loans, by fea-
turing variable payments—low for those who aren't earning
much, then gradually increasing as earnings increase—would go
far toward universalizing access to a college education. Many

people today don't see college as a reasonable option, since the associated debt burden is too high—especially for those who don't get good jobs immediately after graduation.

These changes would be a big step toward establishing the principle that American workers and their children have a right to all the education they need to get ahead. The larger problem of ensuring quality education in all K–12 classes would remain and could be addressed initially through needed, relatively cost-less, educational reforms like increased accountability for results and enhanced choice within the public school system. But re-forming K–12 education will be a lengthy and perhaps expensive process, and the important thing for the Democrats is to make short-term, concrete progress on establishing the principle of ac-cess to all the education people need.

The steps proposed here to expand access to education out-side of the standard K–12 format also have the virtue of speaking to working parents and their difficulties in managing time and child care. Universal preschool takes pressure off providing child care for older preschool children. And a 12/12 school schedule would be a considerable boon to many working parents who have difficulty finding after-school and summer child care, not only by providing high-quality, educationally enriching care but also by considerably simplifying the entire process of juggling work, school, and child-care schedules. This doesn't quite get us to "People who work hard should also be able to spend enough time with their families" and "Women who work outside the home should have access to affordable, quality child care," but it does get us substantially closer to realizing these principles.

Finally, there is the issue of globalization. As the unusually large and vociferous December 1999 protests during the WTO meetings suggested, and as abundant survey data confirm, most Americans, particularly the forgotten majority, are quite nervous about the process of globalization in all its dimensions: ethical, economic, and environmental. Defending the status quo focus on rapidly expanding free trade, no matter what the costs, is just not adequate to addressing these concerns, if it ever was. A way forward for the Democrats, then, is to stress the centrality of minimum labor and environmental standards, including prohibitions on exploitative practices like child labor and guarantees of the rights to organize and bargain collectively. This will not get us immediately to the point where "we all have the right to a decent wage and to speak our minds and organize"—that will take considerable time—but it will help institutionalize the principle involved and ease economic and ethical concerns about globalization.

Strengthening Universalism

We believe the ideas sketched above would be a viable Democratic approach toward reuniting the economic experience of the forgotten majority with their values and thereby attracting their support. And because these are programs whose benefits to forgotten majority voters would be clear and uncontroversial, it would be unusually difficult for the Republicans to effectively counterattack by telling these voters that the programs are just one more example of wasteful and unneeded government spending.

These programs would have another, very important side effect. Because of their universal character, they would be very appealing, indeed, to the base of the Democratic party—blacks, Hispanics, and union household voters—thus providing the bridge that has been missing between that base and forgotten majority voters.

To strengthen that bridge, the Democrats should also consider changing some of their strategies for achieving racial justice. Without in any way compromising their commitment to that value, there are areas in which they could achieve it in ways more consistent with the values of the forgotten majority. Take the use of race-based affirmative action in education—specifically, where it involves clear racial preferences in, for example, college admissions rather than active recruitment of minorities or tie-breaking among equally qualified candidates. It is very difficult intellectually to justify giving a break of hundreds of points on SAT scores to the daughter of upper-middle-class, highly educated blacks and giving nothing remotely similar to the daughter of poor white high school dropouts. And it is very difficult politically to justify such a preference to forgotten majority voters, since it directly violates their core values of fairness and reward for achievement. In fact, race-based admissions policies are increasingly becoming illegal, as one court decision and referendum after another limits the scope of these preferences.

A better approach is *class-based* affirmative action, whereby the poor of all races get a break in consideration for college admissions, reflecting the obstacles they have all overcome in their struggles to better themselves—again, ideally coupled with greater equity across lower levels of public education. This approach still yields considerable racial diversity, since minorities tend to be disproportionately poor and therefore benefit disproportionately from economic preferences.[20] And, in contrast to race-based affirmative action, it brings the interests of the forgotten majority and their minority counterparts together instead of crisply dividing them. Such an approach would help the Democrats underscore the universalist nature of their appeals.

Another commitment the Democrats should consider modifying is race-based school integration. Race-based integration plans, after all, are being struck down all over the country. In addition, they have frequently been unsuccessful in raising achievement rates among minority children because, in city after city—especially outside the South—busing plans have essentially mixed poor blacks and poor whites, an approach that tends to produce few academic gains. A better strategy is to pursue integration by class—that is, to guarantee every child in America the choice to attend a middle-class school. As education expert Richard Kahlenberg argues,[21] this can be done through a modified system of public school choice.

Public school choice is becoming increasingly popular because it provides parents with more options as to where to send their children to school and produces more competition among public schools to attract students, without introducing the difficult and, some argue, dangerous issue of vouchers. Under an intelligently designed public school choice system, the common interests of forgotten majority and minority parents in exercising more choice, avoiding disadvantaged schools, and attending middle-class schools can be brought together instead of being split apart by race. This approach would strengthen universalism and the bridge between white and minority working-class voters that the Democrats need to build.

From Pragmatic Conservatism to Pragmatic Liberalism?

The programs we have outlined have some obvious virtues. They would directly address some key problems of the forgotten majority. They would help institutionalize a series of policy principles that are both supportive of strong government and consistent with the values of the forgotten majority. And they would be popular with the Democratic base.

They would not, however, be inexpensive, which creates a substantial problem. Under the fiscal constraints outlined earlier, there's just not enough money available to fund a series of initiatives of this scale, since almost three-quarters of the surplus is in the lockbox and therefore off-limits.

The obvious solution—and really the only one, in the long run—is to break out of the New Austerity. This means moving away from the lockbox and focusing on the funding of needed programs to attack the New Insecurity. But will the public, particularly the forgotten majority, accept such a focus? These are the same voters, after all, whose pragmatic conservatism has bedeviled the Democrats for years and who have been told over and over that the lockbox is a way of preventing government waste of Social Security dollars.

There are several reasons why this problem is more tractable than it appears over the medium term. The first is that the new economy is leading the way. Given the excellent economic performance of the last several years and the turnaround from chronic deficits to massive surpluses, it is increasingly plausible to argue that America is simply rich enough to afford large-scale programs to solve large-scale problems. Holding back from funding such programs can more and more reasonably be portrayed as excessive fiscal stringency rather than needed fiscal constraint.

Second, public support for current fiscal plans can, to some extent, be read as support for spending, albeit on old rather than new programs. The public does not understand the ins and outs of government accounting, and it supports the Social Security lockbox not because this approach involves debt paydown (this is what mainstream economists like about it) but, rather, because it believes, incorrectly, that the money is somehow being used to make Social Security solvent. So the public is supporting spending, just not on new programs. Similarly, President Clinton's early 1999 proposal to use most of the surplus to shore up Social Security and Medicare—essentially another debt paydown scheme, with the added twist of giving the Social Security and Medicare systems extra government IOUs—got strong public support because it sounded like spending money on two things the public liked: Social Security and Medicare.

Finally, pragmatic conservatism has softened considerably, as we argued earlier. Polling data now typically show forgotten majority support for spending on tax cuts or paying down the national debt running far behind support for spending in areas like education and health care. Forgotten majority voters, in short, are in a spending mood; they're just not sure what specific programs, besides Social Security and Medicare, would be worthwhile investments. If they were sure, we believe they would be quite willing to ignore current fiscal restraints to see such programs implemented. Their conservatism has always been pragmatic; there is no reason why it cannot gradually shift to a sort of pragmatic liberalism.

The shift may take time, however. Demand for new programs has to be built and commitments to the New Austerity gradually eased. Instead, the Democrats, until very recently, have been going in the opposite direction, fetishizing the virtues of budget surplus, strengthening their commitment to fiscal stringency (e.g., accepting the Social Security lockbox), and using their defense of old programs—Medicare and Social Security—to outmaneuver the Republicans in Congress.

The difficulties of switching direction were well illustrated by the early positions of the Democratic presidential candidates, Al Gore and Bill Bradley, in the 2000 election. Both accepted the lockbox. Both restricted their spending proposals to the non–Social Security part of the surplus. And both had agendas that were simultaneously modest and unrealistic—modest because they were restricted to the non–Social Security part of the surplus, unrealistic because they were underfunded relative to what they promised.

Bradley had essentially one new, large-scale program: a complicated effort to make progress on ensuring universal coverage. Slated to cost $65 billion a year, the plan chewed up most of the non–Social Security surplus, leaving Bradley with little room to float other proposals. Since his health care proposal was funded on a level that is generally considered inadequate to obtain just one of its key objectives, universal coverage for children, even if every cent of his proposal was devoted to that one objective,[22] and since it wasn't linked to any other large initiatives, his agenda would have made only a modest dent in the New Insecurity.

Gore did not have one large-scale initiative, but he did have a multiplicity of smaller ones. This was partially because Gore devoted a very substantial portion of the non–Social Security surplus—almost half—to additional debt paydown, this time in the name of Medicare solvency. With what was left, he proposed the following initiatives.

His health-care plan was much more modest that Bradley's, costing $15 billion a year, included a prescription drug benefit for Medicare, and was based primarily on expanding the already-existing Child Health Insurance Program (CHIP). Since CHIP has so far been notably unsuccessful in making progress toward universal coverage for children (in 1998, the number of uninsured children actually increased by 330,000), there is no reason to think an expansion of the program is likely to result in achieving that goal.

Gore also proposed a plan to move toward universal access to preschool for three- and four-year-olds, costing about $5 billion a year. But he acknowledged that the funding was primarily targeted to providing access for four-year-olds only, and that it was dependent, even in this case, on states providing a dollar-for-dollar match with federal contributions. Finally, even with the match from the states, this funding level is probably still not enough to obtain universal access for that age group. Indeed, truly universal preschool for three- and four-year-olds would probably require a commitment large enough[23] to consume all the other funding devoted to education in Gore's campaign proposals.

The rest of his agenda focused on a mix of old favorites (increasing defense spending, providing a fairly large tax cut, hiring more teachers and police officers) and incremental steps toward the new (child-care subsidies, expanding summer school and after-school programs, providing tax-favored 401[j] accounts for education and training, class-size reduction). Needless to say, after the lockbox, the additional chunk of the non–Social Security surplus allocated to debt reduction, and the health-care and universal preschool proposals detailed above, many of these additional initiatives could only be funded at token levels. Thus, while the Gore agenda provided at least something in many areas of concern to forgotten majority voters, the scale of his proposals was unlikely to impress these voters as a serious attack on the New Insecurity. This fact does not bode well for weaning the forgotten majority away from its pragmatic conservatism.

Nor does the fact that both candidates appeared wedded to traditional Democratic support of race-based affirmative action and school desegregation, despite the tenuous legal status of these approaches. Here was a golden opportunity to connect with forgotten majority voters by emphasizing their common, class-based interests with minority voters. But it appears to have been an opportunity lost.

All this Democratic timidity adds up to little change in the New Austerity, little progress on the set of problems these voters have to deal with, little success in changing pragmatic conservatism to pragmatic liberalism, and, we believe, little change in the basic political balance of forces. There is a wild card, though: the possibility of recession. Whether or not it hits in the next presidential term, the advent of an economic downturn will inevitably change the political calculus. The best guess is that a downturn, by intensifying the New Insecurity, will accentuate demand for government action, just as the recession of the early 1990s did. At that point, the less encumbered the Democrats are by the New Austerity and pragmatic conservatism, the better chance they will have to take advantage of an exceptional opportunity to reach the forgotten majority. But they will not be alone, as we explain below.

A Republican Approach

The Republicans face a challenge different from that confronting the Democrats. The Democrats need to transcend pragmatic conservatism in order to mobilize forgotten majority voters and provide them with the sort of programs that would make a real dent in the New Insecurity. The Republicans, on the other hand, depend on pragmatic conservatism for their hold on the forgotten majority. So they need to cultivate this conservatism, at least in a different form, at the same time as they provide their own programs to ease the New Insecurity.

To do this, they need to discard the failed approaches of the post-1994 period that do not appeal to the forgotten majority, starting with the ideological anti-government stance that assumes less government is always good. This view is not shared by forgotten majority voters, who fear that Republican zealots will come after programs they support and need, not just those that truly deserve the axe.

The second big problem is the association of Republicans with an intolerant social conservatism. While forgotten majority voters are not enthusiastic about an aggressive social liberalism, they are even less enthusiastic about perceived Republican attempts to regulate the morality of individual Americans. As we have emphasized throughout this book, such attempts fly in the face of the last thirty years of change in American social values. Republicans would therefore be well advised to turn away from this approach and emphasize their "big tent" credentials instead.

This suggests that George W. Bush's "compassionate conservatism" captures an important element of how the Republicans should appeal to the forgotten majority. They must disassociate themselves from a stridently anti-government and intolerant conservatism, while continuing to build on conservative tendencies in the electorate, particularly among the forgotten majority. The compassionate conservative approach could be a vehicle for doing just that. But it's not enough. As we have emphasized, forgotten majority voters have concerns about their future in the new economy that each party must speak to. Becoming more compassionate and less ideological does not, by itself, speak to those concerns.

In our view, Republicans also need to promote an activist conservatism that takes direct aim at the New Insecurity. For example, there is no reason why Republicans can't advocate substantial investments in education, health care, or retirement security, even as they advocate more choice and decentralization in the system. Indeed, it is when choice policies are seen in competition with adequate funding that Republicans run into trouble. Forgotten majority voters are not so ideologically committed to choice that they are willing to forego such funding, when it is put in an either-or context.

The same could be said of the Republican-led drive to privatize Social Security. This drive has been stymied by voter perception that a private account funded by FICA taxes is in competition with preserving an adequately funded Social Security system. Again, forgotten majority voters will side with adequate funding for a program they support rather than the virtue of being able to exercise more choice. Here, the solution for the Republicans is to advocate private accounts as a *supplement* to an adequately funded system. The same logic applies to Republican attempts to make Medicare into a voucher-based system: More choice should not be linked to a cut in benefits from the system.

Indeed, Republicans should go further and offer their own plans for universalizing health care and pension coverage—plans that combine choice, decentralization, and other Republican themes with a method of attaining these goals. They can't afford to be seen as pooh-poohing these critical forgotten majority problems. Ideology is no substitute for a doctor's visit or a retirement check in these voters' eyes.

Finally, while the Republicans should not give up on tax cuts, these should not appear to compete with adequate funding for programs to alleviate the New Insecurity. Post-1994 political trends suggest strongly that forgotten majority voters are more interested in preserving such funding than in awarding themselves a tax cut. But if these voters can be persuaded that these goals are not in conflict, we think tax cuts can become attractive again to them.

So a successful Republican agenda would include choice, but also investment in education; tax cuts, but also adequate funding for health care. Can this agenda be accomplished within the framework of the New Austerity? No more so than the Democrats could pursue their version of an agenda for the New Insecurity within these constraints.

Indeed, we would argue that the Republican party has a more immediate stake in breaking the austerity regime than the Democrats. At this point, fiscal constraints are so severe that any Republican attempt to cut taxes substantially or spend new money is easily characterized by the Democrats as taking money away from Social Security, Medicare, or some other program that appeals to the forgotten majority. This is intrinsically a losing hand for the Republicans, who are therefore likely to continue to make little political progress until fiscal constraints are loosened.

The problem is well illustrated by George W. Bush's 2000 election campaign. In the early going, the policy centerpiece of Bush's agenda was a proposed $1 trillion tax cut (over ten years), a cut that would pretty much absorb all of the available non–Social Security surplus, if not more than that. Since Bush supported the lockbox, his plan left little money to support initiatives in the areas of education, health, and retirement. For example, even a promising idea like his means-tested vouchers for students in failing schools was only very modestly funded. This made the cautious Democratic approach to the New Insecurity look good by comparison.

John McCain's approach was similarly constrained by an acceptance of the lockbox and a focus on tax cuts. While McCain did not advocate as large a tax cut as Bush—a "mere" $500 billion over ten years—he proposed to use most of the rest of the non–Social Security surplus to fund a transition to a privatized Social Security system (an objective also supported by Bush, though without the additional funding). This left little money to fund new initiatives, and McCain, in fact, proposed none. Again, this approach seemed likely to make the Democrats' mild-mannered approach to the New Insecurity look bold by comparison.

But under loosened constraints, Republicans could offer a real alternative: investment in education *plus* more choice, more retirement security *plus* cutting taxes, and so on. In this way, the Republicans could take a page out of the Democratic playbook and use it for their purposes, instead of the other way around. We believe such an approach could allow the Republicans to expand their appeal to forgotten majority voters and conceivably even break into the Democrats' Hispanic base.

A Reform Party Approach

We have argued that neither party is likely to do a particularly good job mobilizing the forgotten majority in the near term. This creates an opening for the Reform party. Its politics finds a logical home among forgotten majority voters—voters who (as we showed earlier) were the base for Ross Perot's 1992 and 1996 candidacies. (Perot received two-thirds or more of his support in these races from forgotten majority voters.) Minorities, especially blacks, are too closely tied to the Democratic party. And affluent, college-educated whites will find it too difficult to abandon the Republicans and their conservative brand of economics.

But forgotten majority voters wear their loyalties more lightly and may well be attracted again by a movement that "tells it like it is" and speaks directly to their interests, especially if they feel ignored by the major parties. This scenario could lead to the kind of strong electoral performance turned in by Perot in 1992—or perhaps even stronger—which, in turn, could lead to pressure on the two major parties to respond to the issues raised by the Reform party. In that case, American politics in the early 21st century could be quite turbulent, with more surprises like Jesse Ventura's election in 1998 and less of the ho-hum partisan competition that still dominates elections today.

We are not persuaded, however, that a real challenge to the two major parties is likely to emerge anytime soon. The Reform party has already had one of its main economic ideas—fiscal austerity—absorbed by the two major parties and seems to have little to say about the various problems represented by the New Insecurity. The one exception is globalization, but here its prescription—a heavy dose of nativism and protectionism—seems out of step with the priorities of the forgotten majority. This group wants the process of globalization managed, not stopped.

Conclusion

At this point, voters lack faith in *either* party's political-economic approach: The Republicans' seems to consist of eliminating government; the Democrats' seems to consist of a softer, fiscally austere version of the old welfare state. There is little here to stir excitement and partisan commitment, especially among the forgotten majority.

We have argued that this partisan stalemate will continue until such time as the New Austerity is dismantled and the New Insecurity is successfully addressed. The reason is that, *in the long run, the long-run economy matters most.* Just as the Democrats received the blame for the decline of the old New Deal, which dealt a fatal blow to their electoral dominance, so a party—Democrats or Republicans—that receives the *credit* for overcoming the New Insecurity and tapping the full potential of the new economy will be positioned to dominate. Voters will associate the success of the new economic arrangements with that party and reward it accordingly. Those rewards will provide the basis for long-run electoral success, just as they did for Republicans in the Progressive era and for Democrats in the New Deal era.

Until then, the current policy paralysis will continue and the Democrats and Republicans will be reduced to "marketing at the margins"—attempting to cobble together temporary electoral coalitions in a basically unfavorable and dealigned political universe. This makes for neither effective politics nor effective governance, especially when measured against the challenges of a new century. With the support of the forgotten majority, however, we can do better. We can revive active, strong government and build a 21st-century prosperity that is truly inclusive of all Americans.

AFTERWORD

The 2000 Elections
and the Forgotten Majority

RUY TEIXEIRA AND JOEL ROGERS

It was touch and go, but thanks to the quirks of the electoral college and a controversial Supreme Court decision, Republican George W. Bush finally won the 2000 presidential election. In so doing, he received 47.9 percent of the popular vote, quite an improvement over Bob Dole's 40.7 percent in 1996. Of course, Bush did lose the popular vote by half a percentage point to Democrat Al Gore, who received 48.4 percent support in the election, but even that was a substantial improvement over Dole's 1996 deficit of about 8 points. And Bush did this in the face of the Democrats' built-in advantage of being the incumbent party in a period of peace and widespread prosperity.

Where did the Republicans' improved performance in the 2000 election come from? Most fundamentally, from the forgotten majority, which was again decisive in this election. George W. Bush owes his occupancy of the White House to the fact that these voters swung in large numbers into the Republican column in the 2000 election. Without that, the election would not have been close enough for Supreme Court decisions and the other unusual features of the 2000 election to come into play.

Data from the 2000 election clearly support this thesis. First, Bush did very poorly among Democratic base voters. According to the Voter News Service exit poll, blacks supported Gore over Bush by a whopping 90 to 8 percent, an 82 percentage point margin—actually 10 points larger than the Clinton-Dole margin in 1996. In addition, Hispanics supported Gore by a margin of 67 to 31 percent and union household members went for the vice president by 59 to 37 percent. Evidently, the Republican project of cracking the Democratic base—if there was one—was a failure.

Not surprisingly, Bush did generate substantial support from the traditional Republican base of white affluent and highly educated voters. He rolled up a 15 point margin among white voters with more than $75,000 in income (matching Dole's margin in 1996) and a 9 point margin among college-educated whites (somewhat larger than Dole's margin). The key here for Bush was his overwhelming dominance of men from this group. Affluent white men gave Bush 62 percent of their votes and a margin of 28 points over Gore, up from a 20 point Republican lead in 1996. Similarly, college-educated white men gave Bush 61 percent support and a margin of 26 points, up from 17 points in 1996.

But the other side of this picture was Bush's relatively poor performance among affluent and highly educated white women. Among white women with more than $75,000 in household income, Bush received 3 points *less* support than Dole in 1996, losing the group 48–50, where Dole had carried it 51–42. Remarkably, Bush nearly lost the most affluent white women— those with incomes over $100,000—winning them by only 2 points, compared to Dole's 18 point margin in 1996. Bush also lost college-educated white women, by 8 points, a loss that included a stunning 37–59 disadvantage among white women with a postgraduate education. Both figures are comparable to Dole's performance in 1996.

On balance, Bush's performance among the most affluent and highly educated white voters was not impressive when compared to 1996 and does not seem to have been the source of the Republicans' improved performance in 2000. For that, we must turn to voting trends among whites of more modest standing, especially the forgotten majority, where Bush did indeed do much better than Dole in 1996. For example, he won white voters with incomes under $75,000 by 13 points, where Dole in 1996 lost the same group by a point. And Bush carried non-college-educated whites by an impressive 17 points, a group Dole had also lost by a point.

These trends included a strong performance among white working-class women despite Gore's well-documented comeback among those voters after the Democratic convention.[1] Bush wound up carrying white women without a four-year college degree by 7 points, where Dole had lost that group by the same margin. And among white women with incomes under $75,000 Bush held a 2 point lead, up from a 9 point Republican deficit in 1996.

Still, these figures pale in comparison to Bush's most remarkable electoral achievement: his complete domination of white working-class men. Among white men without a four-year degree he received 63 percent support and a whopping 29 point margin over Gore, up from a mere 7 points for Dole. Figures based on income tell a similar story: Bush carried white men with incomes under $75,000 by 23 points, up from an 8 point Republican advantage in 1996. Clearly, Bush was the candidate of the white working class in this election, most especially its male component, who supported him at landslide levels.

But *how* did George W. Bush manage to do so well among forgotten majority voters? Most especially, how did he manage to do so well against Al Gore, a candidate who represented an administration identified with peace and strong economic growth?

Why Gore Didn't Do Better

Some observers argued that the election was Gore's to lose and that he was "too much of a populist," concentrating single-mindedly on programs to help working families. There are several problems with this line of analysis. First, the timing is wrong. Gore's best period in the campaign was by far the month after his speech at the Democratic convention, when his populist profile was sharpest and freshest. And his surge in the final few days before the election coincided with a renewed emphasis on defending Social Security against Bush's privatization plan, a key component of his populist issues package.[2]

Second, "populism"—at least in the mild-mannered Gore version, which consisted chiefly of attacking a small set of corporate special interests widely detested by the public and emphasizing Democratic programs to help working families in areas like Social Security, health and education—was actually quite popular in this election. A *Business Week*/Harris poll taken right after the Democratic convention showed that three-quarters of the public agreed with Gore's attacks on Big Oil, pharmaceutical companies and HMOs. And the VNS exit poll showed Gore winning majorities of the vote on all the issues he emphasized as part of his populist approach. Indeed, among voters who said issues, rather than "qualities," mattered most, Gore ran up a healthy 55–40 margin.

A post-election poll conducted by Greenberg Quinlan Research for the Institute for America's Future fleshes out this picture. The poll shows that core Democratic issue messages around investing the budget surplus in Medicare, Social Security and education, rather than a massive tax cut, were more popular among voters than Bush's basic approach. Voters also preferred Democratic messages around providing prescription drug coverage through Medicare and standing up to HMOs and drug companies. And, very significantly, analysis of the poll data reveals that these

Democratic messages were popular not just among the Democratic base, where one might expect them to be, but also among forgotten majority voters. For example, by 65 to 30 percent non-college-educated whites preferred the Democratic approach to prescription drug coverage, by 51 to 42 percent they preferred the investment-oriented Democratic approach to the budget surplus and by 53 to 41 percent they sympathized with the Democratic message of standing up to HMOs. Not surprisingly, women from this group were more positive about these Democratic messages than their male counterparts were, but among both men and women support for such messages ran 15–20 points ahead of their actual support levels for the Democratic ticket.

Given these data, it seems hard to argue that Gore's populist stance and issue focus delivered the election to Bush, as they had considerable appeal to forgotten majority voters, the very voters among whom Bush made his greatest gains. Gore's approach also clearly helped energize the Democratic base. And it apparently did not turn off the upscale—especially women—judging from the data reviewed earlier. Bush succeeded *despite* Gore's populism, rather than because of it.

Gore's loss has also been attributed to his failure to run strongly on the achievements of the Clinton administration, particularly the long period of robust economic growth and rising incomes. In the extreme version of this argument, usually buttressed by reference to some well-known election forecasting models, the economic situation plus Clinton's high approval ratings should have made it virtually impossible for Gore to avoid winning by a landslide. Therefore, Gore should have ignored voters' problems and focused almost exclusively on cheerleading for the administration's record.

Such a stance was not justified by the strength of the academic models, which are typically based on only a handful of elections. Indeed, economist Ray Fair, whose forecasting model includes no job approval ratings and therefore goes back much farther than the other models, predicted that Gore would win only a bare majority of the popular vote, which of course is what happened. As Fair put it in explaining why his model, based on growth in real per capita disposable income, had such low expectations for candidate Gore: "The economy, while it has been good, is not the best it's ever been. . . . [The growth rate] has been higher in previous elections."

An important paper by political scientists Larry Bartels and John Zaller clarifies this point. They looked at 48 possible election forecasting models using a number of standard variables, including several different economic measures. They then averaged these models' predictions, with each model's weight based on its explanatory power through the 1996 election (a method called "Bayesian weighting"). Since the historically best-performing models tended to be those based on growth in real per capita disposable income, and since there had actually been a slowdown in such growth just prior to the 2000 election, Bartels and Zaller found that the weighted average prediction for Gore's percentage of the two-party popular vote was only half a point off the vote he actually received (as opposed to widely publicized models based on raw economic growth, which predicted anywhere from a 6 point to a 20 point Gore win).

So maybe the economy didn't give Gore such a lock on the election, after all. This seems especially plausible when you factor in the "vice president effect" (the tendency of sitting vice presidents to get relatively little credit for an administration's achievements) and the "Greenspan/new economy effect"(the tendency of the public to credit other factors, like Greenspan and the new economy, more than administration policies for recent prosperity).

Finally, and most important to understanding Bush's victory, the idea that the Clinton record should have been easy to run on flies in the face of the undeniable legacy of the Clinton scandals. Being associated with the scandals—either indirectly, as in the Lewinsky incident, or directly, as in the case of the campaign finance difficulties—clearly made it harder for Gore simply to run on the record of the administration. This is suggested by the fact that nearly two-fifths of voters who gave Clinton a positive job evaluation but disapproved of him as a person wound up voting for Bush.

Why Bush Did So Well

If populism did not hurt Gore and failure to run on the last eight years was not his fatal flaw, what does account for Bush's strong performance, particularly among forgotten majority voters? Here we need to turn to problems of trust, cultural conservatism and generic anti-government sentiment. In the Institute for America's Future poll, these were the most frequently cited doubts about voting for Al Gore. Problems of trust—for example, Gore's "exaggerations and untruthfulness"—were strong among all white voters, a difficulty that had its roots in the Clinton administration's problems but presumably was exacerbated by the flaws in Gore's campaign style. However, problems based on cultural conservatism—chiefly gay marriage, abortion rights and gun control—were notably stronger among non-college-educated whites and among those with incomes under $75,000. In contrast, problems reflecting generic anti-government sentiment—Gore's "support for Federal big government solutions" and the like—were weaker among these voters (even the men) and stronger among the affluent and well-educated.

These findings underscore the brilliance of the Bush strategy. By systematically blurring the differences with his Democratic opponent on crucial policy issues–where voters, including forgotten majority voters, tended to favor the Democrats–Bush was able to bring these other sentiments to the fore. Since Bush also had a prescription drug plan, proposed increases in education and health care spending, pledged to save Medicare and Social Security and supported a patients' bill of rights, confused voters were inclined to choose the candidate they felt more comfortable with from the standpoint of trustworthiness, cultural values or general feelings about government. This was a dynamic that intrinsically favored Bush, as his advisers well knew.

The Institute for America's Future poll shows just how successful Bush's issue-blurring strategy was. While those voters who could form a judgment tended to favor Gore's approach in the areas of education, a patients' bill of rights and prescription drugs, about half (slightly more among forgotten majority voters) could not see enough difference between Gore and Bush to form a judgment. Similarly, over two-fifths of voters could not see enough difference between the candidates' plans to form a judgment on the Social Security issue (also slightly more among forgotten majority voters). This pattern is consistent with a variety of pre-election polls that showed Bush narrowing Gore's issue advantage over the last two months of the campaign as he rolled out his own versions of Democratic programs and emphasized the broad themes of trust, values and big government.

Can the Republicans Hold
Onto the Forgotten Majority?

The evidence suggests that the good results for the Republicans in the 2000 election—hanging onto control of Congress and, of course, winning the presidency—mask substantial underlying weakness, weakness that may threaten their attempts to replicate recent victories. Bush's electoral success was completely dependent on the support of forgotten majority voters who were basically unenthusiastic about his policy ideas and budgetary priorities and who cast their votes more on cultural grounds. Will these voters stick with the Republicans as the memory of the Clinton scandals fades, as Bush (assuming he continues to push his campaign platform) becomes more identified with policy priorities these voters tend not to support and as economic problems intensify demands for government action? There are, to say the least, sufficient grounds for skepticism.

The fact of the matter is that the public opinion climate has changed since the mid-1990s in ways likely to make the Republicans' task of holding onto their forgotten majority support a difficult one. Look at the way elections were fought in 2000—primarily over issues that the Democrats raised: Medicare, social security, prescription drugs, and education. And these issues weren't debated in the typical manner of Republicans arguing that government should do nothing and Democrats insisting that something needed to be done. Instead, candidates from both parties argued over what government should do. The Reagan-era theme—that government is the problem, not the solution—was rarely heard in 2000. Instead of whether to have active government, the debate was over *what kind* of active government to have. The Democrats, as the historic party of active government, enjoy, and will continue to enjoy, a built-in advantage in this debate.

The budgetary situation has also changed in a way that favors the Democrats. In the final chapter of this book, we pointed out how the "new austerity" was handcuffing the Democrats' ability to craft programs that would appeal to forgotten majority voters. But as the new economy continued to deliver higher growth rates and as budget projections were revised in early 2001, it turned out that, even with huge blocs of the surplus committed to debt reduction through the Social Security lockbox, there was still a 10-year total of over $3 trillion potentially available for new initiatives.

House and Senate Democrats may have need of that budgetary room to propose new initiatives. Consider that education was the single issue most cited by voters during the 2000 campaign as their chief concern, yet the Democrats only had a modest 52–44 advantage on the issue in the VNS exit poll. Education was also the economic issue (beside taxes) on which voters most consistently failed to give Gore's approach much, or any, preference over that of Bush. This suggests that defending and extending social insurance, the Democrats' chief emphasis in the 2000 campaign, may not be the way for them to go in the future. While defending social insurance should clearly remain a bedrock commitment of the party, it is difficult to argue that it constitutes a convincing approach to the unfolding problems of the new economy. For many forgotten majority voters, the Democratic approach may have failed to excite for precisely this reason. It may take a more forward-looking approach that focuses on the new economy in critical areas like education, training, child care, work-family stress, scientific research and, of course, health and pension coverage to convince these voters that Democrats really have a vision for the future and their families.

Even with such a forward-looking program, the Democrats will likely continue to meet with resistance on social issues—gun control, gay rights, abortion and the like. However, the solution to these problems is not for Democrats to back away from their basic positions, which are fundamental commitments of the party and are responsible for a good part of their recent success with upscale white women, but to offer these voters a compelling reason to overlook their cultural conservatism—a reason the Gore campaign did not supply but that a forward-looking program could. As the 2000 campaign suggests, soft-pedaling these issues, as Gore did in some ways, does not seem particularly effective in reaching culturally conservative mid- to downscale white voters, especially men.

With such a program, the Democrats' prospects appear excellent. Indeed, looking beneath the surface of the 2000 election results—an election in which, after all, the center-left candidates, Gore and Nader, received 51 percent of the popular vote—an emerging Democratic majority can be discerned. The key elements of this majority would be (1) the Democratic base–chiefly blacks, Hispanics and union households but also including smaller groups like Jews with historic ties to the party; (2) socially liberal upscale white women, particularly in areas where the new economy is emerging; and (3) a majority of mid- to downscale white women and a strong minority of their male counterparts, not particularly socially liberal but attracted to the party by its economic commitments and vision. The 2000 election results suggest that such a majority is possible, but only with more work on the third element and, as we have emphasized, only with a stronger vision and program for the new economy to inspire voters and quell doubts about the party's sometimes controversial social views. We shall see whether the Democrats are up to the task.

Appendix:
Data Sources and
Research Strategy

National Election Studies

The National Election Studies (NES) are biennial academic surveys about politics conducted in every election year by the University of Michigan's Center for Political Studies. The survey has been conducted since 1948 and collects a wide range of data about attitudes, opinions, and voting behavior. The continuity of the survey and the richness of the data make it the premier data source used by academics in the study of American politics.

These factors also contributed to the survey's usefulness to the research conducted for this book. In fact, to the extent that we were interested in political attitudes and the demographics of voting behavior going back to the 1960s, there was really no choice. The NES is the only survey that allows one to go back that far and investigate these issues.

The NES has interviewed between 1,200 and 2,700 respondents over the years. In recent years, the totals have been 2,485 (1992), 1,795 (1994), 1,714 (1996), and 1,281 (1998). Since the NES surveys the adult citizen population, and some adults choose not to vote, the actual number of (self-reported) voters is less than these numbers would suggest. However, even with this diminution of the sample, the survey is quite adequate for looking at broad political and attitudinal trends among voters. For more elaborate analyses of smaller subgroups of the voting electorate (e.g., Hispanics, married working-class whites with children), the NES sample does start to have limitations due to the small number of respondents in such subgroups. But, fortunately, there is an alternative with a much larger sample size, the exit polls (discussed below), that has allowed us to perform these more elaborate analyses for recent elections.

In analyzing the NES (and the exit polls), we have elected to look at the popular vote for president rather than the two-party vote. The reason is that we wanted to look at actual support for the Democrats, and the approach to government they represent, rather than just their success in winning elections. By the latter measure, the Clinton era is really no different from the Kennedy-Johnson era: two presidential elections won by the Democrats in each era. By the former measure, there has been an important shift away from the Democrats and what they represent—a shift that comports well with the general contours of post-1960 political history and attitude trends.

However, one problem with this approach is that the NES does not track the actual popular election results very well. The problem was particularly acute in the elections of 1992 and 1996, when popular support for the Democrats was overestimated by 4–5 percentage points in each election. To get a more accurate sense of how Democratic support among groups like the forgotten majority has actually shifted over time, we therefore reweighted the NES samples to reflect the known outcomes of these elections.

Even then, an additional problem remained: Hardly any change in the popular Democratic vote was apparent when we simply compared the endpoints of our electoral period, 1960 and 1996. On the other hand, after comparing 1964 with 1992, we found a drop-off of 18 percentage points. We elected to combine election surveys in different "eras" to get a sense of how, on average, Democratic support changed from era to era. Specifically, we combined 1960 and 1964 to represent the Kennedy-Johnson era, 1968 and 1972 to represent the Nixon era, 1980 and 1984 to represent the Reagan era, and 1992 and 1996 to represent the Clinton era. At that point we further weighted the NES samples in order to equalize case counts within eras and ensure that one election did not "count" more in our statistical analyses simply because the NES sample was larger during that year.

Bureau of the Census Current Population Survey Voter Supplement

The Current Population Survey (CPS) is the Bureau of the Census's large-scale monthly survey to track changes in the labor market, particularly unemployment rates. In addition, the CPS periodically collects supplementary information about selected social and economic topics. One such effort is the Voter Supplement, administered as part of the November CPS in every election year (both presidential and off-year). The Voter Supplement collects basic information about whether respondents voted, whether they were registered, and a small number of other items (for example, what time of day did the respondent vote?). No information is collected about who the respondents voted for and what their political attitudes and partisan preferences are.

The lack of political information means that the Voter Supplement is useless for examining what any given election is about. But its huge size (90,000 to 100,000 respondents eighteen years of age and over), combined with the rich demographic information that the CPS always collects, makes it a superb source for analyzing how the demographics of the voting pool have changed over time.

As we point out in the text, the Census data indicate, among other things, that the exit polls give a misleading impression of how highly educated voters are. In the 1998 election, for example, the exit polls indicated that 45 percent of voters were college-educated, whereas the Census data indicated that only 31 percent had a four-year college degree. Similarly, in 1996, the exit polls indicated that 43 percent of voters were college-educated, compared to the Census data's figure of 29 percent. These differences are quite substantial, suggesting that the exit polls should be used primarily as they were intended to be used—to project the results of elections—and, secondarily, to compare the political attitudes and preferences of different voter groups.

The question has been raised, most forcefully by political scientists Samuel Popkin and Michael McDonald,[1] as to whether this is a fair judgment, since the Census data are based on self-reports of voting, whereas the exit polls, with all their flaws, are at least based directly on voters. Therefore, perhaps it is the exit poll data that are accurate and the Census data that are biased.

There are a number of things wrong with this argument. The first is that, if one believes the exit poll data, implied turnout levels by education are literally unbelievable. For example, according to the 1996 VRS exit poll, 43 percent of voters were college graduates. But based on the total number of votes cast and the education composition of the population, this figure implies a turnout rate for college graduate citizens of 102 percent—an impossible figure that clearly indicates a serious problem with the exit polls.

Popkin and McDonald have two replies. One is that the exit poll question on education is flawed and that this fact, not education bias in the exit poll sample, accounts for some of the difference between the two surveys. This explanation is correct as far as it goes. The education question on the exit poll typically lists the "some college" category as "some college but no degree." Given this wording, it seems reasonable to assume that some unknown proportion of those with a two-year A.A. degree would bypass this category and select the "college graduate" category instead. This explanation doesn't make the exit polls right; it merely suggests that they overstate the proportion of four-year college graduates for a different reason (the wording of the question instead of sample bias).

Furthermore, the question-wording problem is not nearly enough to account for the discrepancy between the exit poll and Census estimates of the education distribution of voters. Generously assuming that *all* voters with associate degrees are captured by the exit polls' college graduate category, there is still a 5.4 percentage point gap in the number of associate and bachelor's degree holders on the two surveys (43 percent versus 37.6 percent). Note also that the high school–graduate–only category, which is not affected by question-wording discrepancies, also shows substantial upscale education bias (32 percent on the Census survey versus only 24 percent on the exits).

Thus, even under very generous assumptions, there appears to be a serious exit poll sample education bias. Indeed, if we were to assume for a moment that the exit poll data are actually correct, the only way the two surveys could possibly be reconciled would be through vastly higher misreporting by lower-education respondents in the Census data. But this approach would run smack up against analyses of validated vote data from the Michigan National Election Study (NES) that show exactly the reverse. That is, according to a 1986 article by political scientists Brian Silver, Barbara Anderson, and Paul Abramson,[2] *high-education respondents are much more likely, not less likely, to overreport voting*. In short, self-reporting by low-education respondents in the Census survey is an unlikely source for a such a large downscale bias in the Census data.

Popkin and McDonald counter by pointing out that nonvoting is so common among low-education respondents that even lower misreporting by such respondents could still produce a downscale bias. This conclusion is correct, but Popkin and McDonald never estimate how much downscale bias could possibly be produced by such misreporting. We examined this possibility and found that, even under extreme assumptions, misreporting by low-education respondents, using the relative rates estimated by Silver, Anderson, and Abramson, could account for only 1 percentage point of the difference between the exit poll data and the Census data. We conclude that the exit poll sample education bias is real and, combined with the flawed question wording, leads to the exit polls' radical overstatement of the proportion of highly educated voters.

National Exit Polls

A consortium of television networks and newspapers sponsors large national exit polls during every presidential and off-year election, currently conducted by Voter News Service (VNS). The questions asked are fewer in number than those asked by the NES, but the sample size is much larger (11,000 to 16,000 voters in recent years, compared to just 700 to 1700 for the NES). Thus, the VNS is an ideal data source for looking at recent trends in voting support among various demographic subgroups.

However, as we have argued, it is not a good source for looking at the demographic composition of voters, especially variables related to education. In cases where we have needed to use the exit polls for this purpose (see Table 5.1), we reweighted the exit polls to reflect the education distribution among voters indicated by the Census data.

NOTES

Preface

1. William Booth, "With a New Script, the Action's in the Middle," *Washington Post*, June 27, 1999, p. A1.

Chapter One

1. For data generally supporting this analysis, see Everett Carll Ladd, Jr., and Charles Hadley, *Transformations of the American Party System: Political Coalitions from the New Deal to the 1970's* (New York: Norton, 1975), chapters 1 and 2. Note, however, that Ladd and Hadley do not typically break down the electorate by class and race but, rather, give voting rates by class and race in New Deal elections. Nevertheless, given what we know about the demographics of the country at the time, these voting rates allow us to make reasonable inferences about who comprised the voting electorate and where the Democrats' support base lay in these elections.

2. For a good description of this evolution in attitudes toward liberalism, see Thomas Edsall and Mary D. Edsall, *Chain Reaction: The Impact of Race, Rights and Taxes on American Politics* (New York: Norton, 1991), chapters 3 and 4.

3. Council of Economic Advisors, *Economic Report of the President* (Washington, D.C.: Government Printing Office, 1999).

4. These figures are based on the authors' analysis of the 1998 Current Population Survey (CPS) Outgoing Rotation Group (ORG) data.

5. See Stephen A. Herzenberg, John A. Alic, and Howard Wial, *New Rules for a New Economy: Employment and Opportunity in Postindustrial America* (Ithaca, N.Y.: Cornell University Press, 1998), not just for stylized facts

like these but also for a careful analysis of service-favoring employment trends, associated problems, and policy measures to solve them.

6. Statistical Abstract of the United States (Washington, D.C.: Bureau of the Census, 1998); authors' analysis of 1996 CPS data.

7. International Monetary Fund, *World Economic Outlook* (Washington, D.C.: IMF, 1998).

8. This estimate is based on Economic Policy Institute (EPI) analyses of CPS data, 1984–97.

9. Jeffrey Madrick, *The End of Affluence: The Causes and Consequences of America's Economic Dilemma* (New York: Random House, 1995).

10. This figure, stated in 1998 dollars, is based on extrapolation from available data on forgotten majority income levels in 1979 and income trends among all whites from 1973 to 1979.

11. The year 1999 is the latest one for which these particular data are available.

12. Henceforth, we shall mean a four-year college degree when we use the phrase *college degree* without qualification. The wage and income levels of people with two-year college degrees (A.A.s) are much more similar to those of people with some college, but no degree, than to those of people with four-year degrees.

13. Throughout this volume, when we refer to wages, incomes, and other quantities denominated in dollars, we mean *real* dollars—that is, dollars adjusted for inflation. And in cases where data do not refer to a trend, we specify the year that the real dollars are in (e.g., 1998 dollars).

14. All data on wage trends by education were taken from Lawrence Mishel, Jared Bernstein, and John Schmitt, *The State of Working America 2000–2001* (Armonk, N.Y.: M. E. Sharpe, 2001).

15. Based on the Bureau of Labor Statistics data series on average hourly wages for production and nonsupervisory workers. Median hourly wage data, which would be a better measure, are not available before 1973.

16. These figures are stated in 1998 dollars. See Edith Rasell, Barry Bluestone, and Lawrence Mishel, *The Prosperity Gap: A Chartbook of American Living Standards* (Washington, D.C.: Economic Policy Institute, 1997); and authors' calculations. More detail on these economic trends is contained in Lawrence Mishel, Jared Bernstein, and John Schmitt, *The State of Working America 1996–97* (Armonk, N.Y.: M. E. Sharpe, 1997), and Lawrence Mishel, Jared Bernstein, and John Schmitt, *The State of Working America 1998–99* (Armonk, N.Y.: M. E. Sharpe, 1999).

17. Besides the very tangible reality of the Great Divide, there are good reasons to define the white working class in this way. *Education data* are almost always collected with political surveys, and the educational categories used are usually commensurate across surveys. Moreover, education data are typically collected on all survey respondents, not just those who currently hold a job, so it is possible to categorize all individuals in the survey. *Occupation data*, on the other hand, though they more directly tap the traditional definition of "working class," are frequently not collected on political surveys. And when they are, the categories used vary wildly and typically leave out those people not holding a job, or even all those not holding a full-time job. *Income data* are more commonly collected on political surveys. However, these data are usually categorical and the categories vary substantially across surveys. And then there is the problem of inflation, which makes comparison of categorical income data from different time periods very problematic. Of course, some might argue that, since the typical non-college-educated white has a moderate income and a moderate level of education and does not work in a blue-collar job, this person should be categorized as "middle class." After all, don't almost all Americans, given the opportunity, describe themselves as middle class? The answer is "yes"—but only if no "working class" choice is offered. When the question is asked with a wider range of choices, *including* a working-class choice, roughly equal numbers of all respondents say they are working class or middle class and, *among whites without a four-year college degree, a clear majority say they are working class rather than middle class* (based on the authors' analysis of National Election Study data, plus data from S. M. Miller and Karen Marie Ferroggiaro, "Class Dismissed," *The American Prospect* 21 [1995]: 100–104), and Roper Center, "Everyday Life: A Roper Center Data Review," *The Public Perspective*, April/May, 1999). So the designation "working class" is hardly foreign to the group we're talking about.

18. Note that this figure would not be much different if an occupation-based definition of "working class" were used; figured across the adult workforce, the percentage of workers who are non-college-educated whites is about the same as the percentage of workers who are whites without professional or managerial positions.

19. These figures are based on the authors' analysis of 1998 CPS Outgoing Rotation Group data.

20. These figures, stated in 1998 dollars, are based on the authors' analysis of the March 1998 CPS data.

21. For a discussion of middle-class income levels, see Frank Levy, *The New Dollars and Dreams: American Incomes and Economic Change* (New York: Russell Sage Foundation, 1998).

22. These figures are based on the authors' analysis of March 1998 CPS data. Figures are in 1998 dollars.

23. These occupation and industry figures are based on the authors' analysis of the 1998 CPS Outgoing Rotation Group data.

24. These figures are stated in 1998 dollars, based on unpublished 1996 CPS data provided to the authors by Stephen Rose.

25. Among the adult individuals identified on the CPS public-use tapes as residing in the suburbs, about 14 percent are not identified spatially beyond metropolitan/nonmetropolitan status due to confidentiality considerations.

26. Ben Wattenberg, *Values Matter Most* (New York: Free Press, 1995).

27. See Arthur H. Miller, Anne Hildreth, and Christopher Wlezien, "Social Group Dynamics of Political Evaluations," paper delivered at the annual meeting of the Midwestern Political Science Association, Chicago, 1988. This paper is well summarized in William Mayer, *The Changing American Mind: How and Why American Public Opinion Changed Between 1960 and 1988* (Ann Arbor: University of Michigan Press, 1992), chapter 12, which contains additional useful details on the evolution of activist government's image.

Chapter Two

1. William Galston and Elaine Kamarck, "5 Realities That Will Shape 21st Century Politics," *Blueprint: Ideas for a New Century* (Washington, D.C: Democratic Leadership Council, Fall 1998).

2. We use the term *demographic* here in the loose sense of an objective, rather than attitudinal, characteristic of an individual; that is, we are treating everything from marital status to spatial location to occupation to educational attainment as a demographic characteristic. Demographers, of course, use a much stricter definition.

3. William G. Mayer, *The Changing American Mind: How and Why American Public Opinion Changed Between 1960 and 1988* (Ann Arbor: University of Michigan Press, 1992).

4. This figure is based on the Census Bureau's central city–metro (urban)/noncentral city–metro (suburban)/nonmetro (rural) break-

down, as cited in Census Bureau Historical Poverty Table 8 on the bureau's website.

5. Using a shift-share analysis, one can estimate the change that would occur in a particular outcome of interest—here, the Democratic vote—if nothing had changed save the share of the population in different demographic categories—here, suburbs versus cities versus rural areas. In the present context, our analysis is based on National Election Studies (NES) data.

6. Here we mean the massive increase among voters. (Note, however, that the trend in distrust of government among the general public is no different, as we show later in the chapter.)

7. See Seymour Martin Lipset, *Political Man: The Social Bases of Politics* (Baltimore: Johns Hopkins University Press, 1981), for the classic statement of this argument.

8. Our analysis indicates that the National Election Studies cumulative file category labeled "professional and managerial" actually includes, besides professionals and managers, those people generally labeled "technicians and related support" in Census occupational classifications. However, given the small changes in the size of this latter category over time—based on official Census data—the shift in the NES category, even with this flaw, should overwhelmingly measure change among professionals and managers, properly defined.

9. Based on shift-share analyses of National Election Studies data.

10. Bureau of Labor Statistics (BLS) data show a shift of about 10 percentage points toward professional-managerial-technical work between 1960 and 1996 among employed persons. The corresponding figure in the NES is *15* percentage points, 50 percent higher than the BLS figure.

11. For a clear, if thinly supported, statement of this position, see William Galston and Elaine Kamarck, "5 Realities That Will Shape 21st Century Politics," *Blueprint: Ideas for a New Century* (Washington, D.C.: Democratic Leadership Council, Fall 1998).

12. Anthony Carnevale and Stephen Rose, *Education for What? The New Office Economy* (Washington, D.C.: Educational Testing Service, 1998).

13. And one-half of supervisors. (See *Education for What? The New Office Economy* for an explanation of this coding decision.)

14. All of the data in this paragraph and the next one are based on the authors' analysis of NES data, utilizing code that was kindly provided by Stephen Rose to map NES occupation and industry categories into his functional categories.

15. Indeed, based on these relative support rates for the Democrats, the effect of the growth of the new economy should have been to *increase* support for the Democrats, since workers have shifted out of the Factory into two sectors (the Office and the Hospital/Classroom) where Democratic support is higher, at least at this point. Of course, in all likelihood, these relationships were reversed in the early 1960s, suggesting, once again, the centrality of changes *within* groups like factory workers, rather than the shifts *between* different groups of workers.

16. Note that those with some college are much closer in wages and income to high school graduates than to those with a four-year college degree. Their post-1973 wage and income trends also closely parallel those of high school graduates—specifically in terms of declining wages and stagnating incomes. (See Lawrence Mishel, Jared Bernstein, and John Schmitt, *The State of Working America, 1998–99* [Armonk, N.Y.: M. E. Sharpe, 1999], chapter 3, for detailed data.) In many important respects, those with some college are more usefully treated as souped-up high school graduates than as "college-educated" individuals, given the large disparities between their economic status and that of four-year college graduates. In that sense, of course, they should be natural material for the Democrats.

17. The proportion of high school graduates among white voters remained roughly constant.

18. Specifically, shift-share calculations.

19. Daniel Yankelovich, "How Changes in the Economy Are Reshaping American Values," in Henry J. Arron, Thomas E. Mann, and Timothy Taylor, eds., *Values and Public Policy* (Washington, D.C.: Brookings, 1994).

20. See Table 4-1 in Everett C. Ladd and Karlyn H. Bowman, *What's Wrong: A Survey of American Satisfaction and Complaint* (Washington, D.C.: AEI Press, 1998).

21. Here the picture is more mixed. For analysis and discussion, see the section titled "Are Americans More Ideologically Conservative?" later in this chapter.

22. See Tom W. Smith, "Liberal and Conservative Trends in the United States Since World War II," *Public Opinion Quarterly* 54 (1990): 479–507; James A. Davis, "Changeable Weather in a Cooling Climate Atop the Liberal Plateau," *Public Opinion Quarterly* 56 (1992): 261–306; and James A. Davis, "The GSS: Capturing American Attitude Change," *Public Perspective* 8, no. 2 (February-March 1997): 31–34.

23. See Table 3.15 in William G. Mayer, *The Changing American Mind: How and Why American Public Opinion Changed Between 1960 and 1988* (Ann Arbor: University of Michigan Press, 1992).

24. Clem Brooks, "Civil Rights Liberalism and the Suppression of a Republican Political Realignment in the U.S., 1972–96," unpublished manuscript, Department of Sociology, Indiana University, Bloomington, 1998.

25. Changes in policy attitudes toward black civil rights have played a similar, though smaller, role in the last several decades. See the next section in this chapter for further discussion.

26. Ronald Inglehart, *The Silent Revolution: Changing Values and Political Styles Among Western Publics* (Princeton: Princeton University Press, 1971), and Ronald Inglehart, "The Silent Revolution in Europe: Intergenerational Change in Post-Industrial Societies," *American Political Science Review* 65 (1977): 991–1017.

27. James A. Davis, "Review of Value Change in Global Perspective," *Public Opinion Quarterly* 60 (1996): 322–331.

28. For further critiques along these lines, see Clem Brooks and Jeff Manza, "Do Changing Values Explain the New Politics? A Critical Assessment of the Postmaterialist Thesis," *Sociological Quarterly* 35 (1994): 541–570, and Harold D. Clarke, Nitish Dutt, and Jonathan Rapkin, "Conversations in Context: The (Mis)Measurement of Value Change in Advanced Industrial Societies," unpublished manuscript, Department of Political Science, University of Texas, 1996.

29. Interestingly enough, in comparing *nonwhites* to whites, instead of blacks to whites, one also finds a large decline in the nonwhite Democratic presidential vote. But this is simply a "mix effect" reflecting the increasing weight of nonblacks (e.g., Hispanics, Asians) who, in the minority population, vote Democratic at rates far below blacks.

30. The source for the first example in this paragraph is Stephen Thernstrom and Abigail Thernstrom, *America in Black and White: One Nation Indivisible* (New York: Simon and Schuster, 1997). All of the other examples are cited from William G. Mayer, *The Changing American Mind: How and Why American Public Opinion Changed Between 1960 and 1988* (Ann Arbor: University of Michigan Press, 1992), appendix B.

31. For more examples and discussion, see William G. Mayer, *The Changing American Mind: How and Why American Public Opinion Changed Between 1960 and 1988* (Ann Arbor: University of Michigan Press, 1992), and Stephen Thernstrom and Abigail Thernstrom, *America in Black*

and White: One Nation Indivisible (New York: Simon and Schuster, 1997).

32. Tom W. Smith, "Liberal and Conservative Trends in the United States Since World War II," *Public Opinion Quarterly* 54 (1990): 479–507, and James A. Davis, "Changeable Weather in a Cooling Climate Atop the Liberal Plateau," *Public Opinion Quarterly* 56 (1992): 261–306.

33. Clem Brooks, "Civil Rights Liberalism and the Suppression of a Republican Political Realignment in the U.S., 1972–96," unpublished manuscript, Department of Sociology, Indiana University, Bloomington, 1998.

34. Donald Kinder and Lynn Sanders, *Divided by Color: Racial Politics and Democratic Ideals* (Chicago: University of Chicago Press, 1996).

35. Paul M. Sniderman, Edward G. Carmines, William Howell, and Will Morgan, "A Test of Alternative Interpretations of the Contemporary Politics of Race: A Critical Examination of *Divided by Color*," paper presented at the Midwest Political Science Association annual meeting, Chicago, 1997. Paul Sniderman further develops his analysis of race and politics in two important co-authored books, Paul M. Sniderman and Thomas Piazza, *The Scar of Race* (Cambridge, Mass.: Harvard University Press, 1993), and Paul M. Sniderman and Edward G. Carmines, *Reaching Beyond Race* (Cambridge, Mass.: Harvard University Press, 1997).

36. Martin Gilens, *Why Americans Hate Welfare: Race, Media, and the Politics of Antipoverty Policy* (Chicago: University of Chicago Press, 1999).

37. As well as spending on most other welfare state programs, from health, education, and Social Security to a wide variety of programs to help the poor. Of course, faith in the *efficacy* of such spending is a different matter. See the next section for a detailed discussion not only of trends in support of welfare state spending but also of this crucial distinction between support for spending and belief in the effectiveness of spending.

38. Edward G. Carmines and James A. Stimson, *Issue Evolution: Race and the Transformation of American Politics* (Princeton: Princeton University Press, 1989); Thomas B. Edsall and Mary Edsall, *Chain Reaction: The Impact of Race, Rights and Taxes on American Politics* (New York: W. W. Norton, 1991).

39. Alan Abramowitz, "Issue Evolution Reconsidered: Racial Attitudes and Partisanship in the U.S. Electorate," *American Journal of Political Science* 38 (1994): 1–24.

40. Paul M. Sniderman, Edward G. Carmines, William Howell, and Will Morgan, "A Test of Alternative Interpretations of the Contemporary

Politics of Race: A Critical Examination of *Divided by Color*," paper presented at the Midwest Political Science Association annual meeting, Chicago, 1997; Martin Gilens, *Why Americans Hate Welfare: Race, Media, and the Politics of Antipoverty Policy* (Chicago: University of Chicago Press, 1999).

41. This year, 1972, was the first in which the NES asked the ideology question, so we were unable to return to the 1960–64 era and perform the same type of shift-share analyses that we did earlier in this chapter.

42. Alan Abramowitz and Kyle Saunders, "Ideological Alignment in the U.S. Electorate," unpublished manuscript, Emory University, Department of Political Science, 1997; Kathleen Knight and Robert S. Erikson, "Ideology in the 1990s," in Barbara Norrander and Clyde Wilcox, eds., *Understanding Public Opinion* (Washington, D.C.: Congressional Quarterly Press, 1997).

43. Among those who ventured an opinion. (Note that the inclusion of nonsubstantive responses had almost no effect on the time trend in trust in government discussed here.)

44. Poll readings since the 1996 election show little evidence of change in this measure. (See the massive time-series table in Everett C. Ladd and Karlyn H. Bowman, *What's Wrong: A Survey of American Satisfaction and Complaint* [Washington, D.C.: AEI Press, 1998].) The average proportion of people who indicated their trust in the government over eight postelection readings is very close to the 1996 NES reading.

45. These data were taken from the tables in chapter 5 of Everett C. Ladd and Karlyn H. Bowman, *What's Wrong: A Survey of American Satisfaction and Complaint* (Washington, D.C.: AEI Press, 1998). The specific figures mentioned reflect the latest poll readings contained in the relevant table.

46. William G. Mayer, *The Changing American Mind: How and Why American Public Opinion Changed Between 1960 and 1988* (Ann Arbor: University of Michigan Press, 1992).

47. Mayer is currently updating his analysis to include the 1990s.

48. Clem Brooks, "The Decline of Liberalism? Explaining Trends in American Ideological Identifications, 1972–1994," unpublished manuscript, Department of Sociology, Indiana University, Bloomington, Indiana, 1997.

49. Pew Research Center, *Deconstructing Distrust: How Americans View Government* (Washington, D.C.: Pew Research Center for the People and the Press, 1998).

50. William G. Mayer, *The Changing American Mind: How and Why American Public Opinion Changed Between 1960 and 1988* (Ann Arbor: University of Michigan Press, 1992). James Stimson, in *Public Opinion in America: Moods, Cycles and Swings* (Boulder, Colo.: Westview, 1991), goes so far as to argue for the emergence of a full-throated liberal "mood" in the 1980s, equivalent to Kennedy-Johnson era liberalism. This, of course, runs completely contrary to the image most harbor of the Reagan-Bush era. While Stimson's results, based on a fairly elaborate statistical exercise, appear to be driven somewhat by his choice of questions, most public opinion analysts agree with the basic point that the 1980s witnessed a liberal resurgence in many areas of public opinion—though they would stop short of embracing Stimson's view about the magnitude of this shift.

51. Tom W. Smith, "Public Support for Public Spending, 1974–1994," *The Public Perspective* (April/May 1995), and Tom W. Smith, "Trends in National Spending Priorities, 1973–1998," unpublished manuscript, National Opinion Research Center, Chicago, 1999.

52. See Martin Gilens, *Why Americans Hate Welfare: Race, Media, and the Politics of Antipoverty Policy* (Chicago: University of Chicago Press, 1999), for a review of data on public support for social spending that reaches the same basic conclusion.

53. *Domestic social spending* is defined by Smith as covering the following areas: health, education, welfare, solving the problems of the big cities, and improving the conditions of blacks.

54. *Household income* here refers to the household income of *individuals* eighteen and over; note that this definition is different from the one used by the Census Bureau, based on the household unit.

55. The latest year available for wage data on the forgotten majority is 1998; the latest year available for income data on the forgotten majority is also 1998.

56. All figures in this paragraph are stated in 1998 dollars.

57. See Frank Levy, *The New Dollars and Dreams: American Incomes and Economic Change* (New York: Russell Sage Foundation, 1998).

58. All of these figures from Levy's *The New Dollars and Dreams* are stated in 1997 dollars.

59. Lawrence Mishel, Jared Bernstein, and John Schmitt, *The State of Working America, 1998–99* (Ithaca, N.Y.: Cornell University Press, 1999).

60. This annual rate holds true whether measured at the median through Current Population Survey (CPS) data or through the BLS's production/nonsupervisory worker wage series.

61. Jennifer Campbell, *Health Insurance Coverage: 1998*. Bureau of the Census: Report P60-208 (October 1999).

62. The Gini ratio, a standard measure of inequality, is now very close to its post–World War II high.

63. The top is defined as the 90th percentile of the wage distribution; the middle is defined as the 50th percentile (median) of the wage distribution.

64. No data are available before 1973.

65. See Pew Research Center, *Retropolitics, The Political Typology: Version 3.0* (Washington, D.C.: Pew Research Center, 1999), and Andrew Kohut, "Globalization and the Wage Gap," *New York Times,* December 3, 1999, p. A31.

66. See James Stimson, *Public Opinion in America: Moods, Cycles and Swings* (Boulder, Colo.: Westview, 1991), chapter 2, for a useful discussion of values and value trade-offs in political conflict.

67. See David G. Lawrence, *The Collapse of the Democratic Presidential Majority* (Boulder, Colo.: Westview, 1997). Lawrence also shows that the rise of Reagan and perceived extremism in the Republican party largely eliminated the Democratic disadvantage in this area. Unfortunately for the Democrats, as Lawrence further shows, this disadvantage was replaced with one just as serious in the area of economic management.

Chapter Three

1. This particular quote is taken from Wattenberg's summary of his book on the American Enterprise Institute website.

2. For an interesting scholarly overview of the formation and evolution of the DLC, see Jon F. Hale, "The Making of the New Democrats," *Political Science Quarterly* 110, no. 2 (1995): 207–232.

3. See William Galston and Elaine Kamarck, *The Politics of Evasion* (Washington, D.C.: Progressive Policy Institute, 1989), for a classic statement of this position, as well as for the quote (pp. 27–28) cited in the text.

4. See the account in John Judis, "The New Beginning," unpublished manuscript, The Wilson Center, Washington, D.C., 1999.

5. Initially, in an article in *The New Republic,* and also in his book *The Paradox of American Democracy: Elites, Special Interests and the Betrayal of Public Trust* (New York: Pantheon, 2000).

6. In his October 1992 speech in Raleigh, N.C., Clinton laid out his basic announced approach.

7. For some evidence on the electorate's unusually negative evaluations of Bush and the Republicans in 1992, see Paul R. Abramson, John H. Aldrich, and David W. Rohde, *Change and Continuity in the 1992 Elections* (Washington, D.C.: Congressional Quarterly Press, 1994), chapter 7.

8. While we are primarily interested in the popular vote for Clinton, as an indicator of support for his and the Democrats' brand of activist government, it should be noted that the Voter Research and Surveys (VRS) exit poll found that Perot voters would have split their vote about evenly between Clinton and Bush—suggesting a Clinton victory even if Perot had not run. However, Everett C. Ladd, "The 1992 Vote for President Clinton: Another Brittle Mandate?" *Political Science Quarterly* 108, no. 1 (1993): 1–29, and others, objected strenuously to this suggestion, arguing that Perot's entry into the race and relentless attacks on the incumbent altered the campaign dynamic decisively in Clinton's favor. This dispute aside, the fact is that Perot *did* run, and enormous numbers of anti-Bush voters (including half of all Bush defectors) chose to vote for a maverick Texas billionaire rather than for the nominee of the Democratic party. It is therefore hard to interpret the popular vote totals as indicating anything other than Democratic electoral weakness.

9. No comparisons to 1988 are available due to category incompatibility.

10. See Judis's excellent analysis of the Perot phenomenon and the Reform party in *The American Prospect*, November 23, 1999.

11. Specifically, Current Population Survey (CPS) wage data merged with the 1992 VRS exit poll.

12. For some comparative data on wage losses among all Perot and Clinton voters over various time periods, see Ruy A. Teixeira, *The Politics of the High Wage Path: The Challenge Facing Democrats,* Working Paper (Washington, D.C.: Economic Policy Institute, 1994), table 3.

13. To avoid awkward and tedious phrasing in what follows, we refer to wage trends among groups that voters belong to as, simply, wage trends among those voters; for example, "Perot voters lost 10 percent in real wages" instead of "Perot voters belonged to groups that lost 10 percent in real wages."

14. For more data and discussion on Perot voters and economic nationalism, see Ruy A. Teixeira and Guy Molyneux, *Economic Nationalism and the Future of American Politics* (Washington, D.C.: Economic Policy Institute, 1994).

15. These data were drawn from 1992 VRS exit poll results.

16. This part of the discussion draws on Stanley Greenberg's very useful study of Perot voters, *The Road to Realignment* (Washington, D.C.: Democratic Leadership Council, 1993).

17. This poll was conducted by Stanley Greenberg for the Democratic Leadership Council. The results are presented in *The Road to Realignment* (Washington, D.C.: Democratic Leadership Council, 1993).

18. Stanley Greenberg, *Middle Class Dreams: The Politics and Power of the New American Majority* (New York: Times Books, 1995).

19. Todd Schafer, "Still Neglecting Public Investment" (Washington, D.C.: Economic Policy Institute, 1993).

20. Gallup-CNN poll, November 1993.

21. See Theda Skocpol, *Boomerang: Clinton's Health Security Effort and the Turn Against Government in U.S. Politics* (New York: W. W. Norton, 1996), and John Judis, *The Paradox of American Democracy: Elites, Special Interests and the Betrayal of Public Trust* (New York: Pantheon, 2000).

22. For an exceptionally clear and thoughtful argument stating that what the administration did was both desirable and inevitable, see Jonathan Chait, "Clinton's Bequest: The Progressive Uses of Fiscal Conservatism," *The American Prospect*, December 6, 1999.

23. This trend was composed of two different changes: an income drop in 1992–93 and an income rise in 1993–94. But the net result was a .3 percent decline over the two years.

24. Mostly those with a four-year college degree. Note, however, that due to ambiguous wording in Voter News Service (VNS) questions, this category contains an undetermined number of individuals with two-year associate's degrees. For more discussion, see the Appendix.

25. VNS poll.

26. See Ruy Teixeira, *The Politics of the High Wage Path: The Challenge Facing Democrats*, Working Paper (Washington, D.C.: Economic Policy Institute, 1994); Ruy Teixeira, "The Real Electorate," *The American Prospect* 37 (March-April 1998); and the Appendix.

27. November 1994 CPS Voter Supplement data.

28. Based on the authors' analysis of CPS wage data cross-linked to VNS exit poll data.

29. See Fred Steeper, *This Swing Is Different: Analysis of the 1994 Election Exit Polls* (Southfield, Mich.: Market Strategies, 1995), for the most detailed explication of this viewpoint.

30. 1994 VNS exit poll; 1990 VRS exit poll; 1988 CBS/*New York Times* exit poll; 1984 CBS/*New York Times* exit poll. See also Pew Research Center,

Poll Watch: January 3, 1996 (Washington, D.C., 1996), for supportive data on the relative stability of conservative self-identification in the electorate. The Pew Center data, drawn from CBS/*New York Times* and *Los Angeles Times* national polls, go back to 1977 and 1980, respectively.

31. A standard ordinary least squares (OLS) model was estimated on both the 1992 and 1994 exit poll data and included (a) standard demographics (education, income, age, marital status, religion, race, and sex); (b) assessments of both national and personal economic situations; and (c) partisanship and ideology. (See Ruy Teixeira and Joel Rogers, "Volatile Voters: Declining Living Standards and Non-College-Educated Whites," Working Paper 116 [Washington, D.C.: Economic Policy Institute, August 8, 1996], appendix 2, for detailed results.) The model was also estimated using a maximum likelihood estimate procedure, or probit. The pattern of results from this probit model mimicked the OLS results.

32. This shift was also signaled on the descriptive level: The percentage of independents voting democratic for the House dropped 11 points between 1992 and 1994. For some reason, however, this shift was generally ignored in postelection analyses, while the shift among conservatives got a good amount of attention.

33. Differences in coefficients were tested by pooling the data from the two years and estimating interaction effects between variables and a year dummy for 1994. For conservatism, the interaction effect had a magnitude of .0015 and a standard error of .024. This produced a t-statistic of .064, which translates into a significance level of .9493—very insignificant, indeed.

34. This analysis was performed using a standard Oaxaca decomposition procedure on the basic House vote models, as shown in appendix 2 of Ruy Teixeira and Joel Rogers, "Volatile Voters: Declining Living Standards and Non-College-Educated Whites," Working Paper 116 (Washington, D.C.: Economic Policy Institute, August 8, 1996).

35. Ben Wattenberg, *Values Matter Most* (New York: Free Press, 1995).

36. Wattenberg also included education as a key values issue; however, we believe that this inclusion is not justified, given that education has such a huge economic component, whether viewed from the standpoint of society or from that of individuals and families. Certainly education fits in poorly with crime, welfare, and affirmative action as a primarily "values" issue.

37. Ben Wattenberg, "President Vows to Get It Right This Time," *Washington Times*, November 2, 1995.

38. This conclusion is based on the 1994 OLS model cited previously, with a variable for mentioning crime added to the model. See also Michael Hagen, "The Crime Issue and the 1994 Elections," paper presented at the 1995 American Political Science Association Annual Meeting, 1995, for evidence on the weakness of crime as a voting issue, not only in 1994, but in previous elections as well.

39. These findings are based on the authors' analysis of November 1994 CPS Voter Supplement data. Note, however, that the CPS data overstate the actual level of turnout among any demographic group due to overreporting by survey respondents. For example, the overall level of turnout reported in the November 1994 CPS was 44.6 percent, compared to the actual turnout level of 38.8 percent, as compiled from official data (Non-Voter Study, Committee for the Study of the American Electorate, Washington, D.C., 1995). And, correcting for this overreporting, we estimate that the turnout of poor voters was closer to 26 percent than to the 30 percent reported in the CPS data.

40. See Ruy Teixeira, *The Disappearing American Voter* (Washington, D.C.: Brookings, 1992), for a recent discussion, and Walter Dean Burnham, *The Current Crisis of American Politics* (New York: Oxford University Press, 1982), for historical context.

41. 1994 VNS exit poll.

42. That is, overreporting in the 1990 survey was relatively high, thereby artificially increasing the amount of turnout decline measured by the 1994 survey. Correcting for this differential overreporting suggests a decline in poor turnout of 2.3, not 5, percentage points.

43. This conclusion is based on simple simulations combining data from the 1994 VRS exit poll with the Census data.

44. Non-Voter Study, Committee for the Study of the American Electorate, Washington, D.C., 1995.

45. See also Alfred J. Tuchfarber, Stephen Bennett, Andrew Smith, and Eric Rademacher, "The Republican Tidal Wave of 1994: Testing Hypotheses About Realignment, Restructuring and Rebellion," *PS: Political Science and Politics* 28 (1995): 689–696, for an analysis of the differential turnout argument that comes to a similar conclusion using different data and a different methodology.

46. See Stanley Greenberg's postelection poll for the Democratic Leadership Council in Stanley Greenberg, *The Revolt Against Politics* (Washington, D.C.: Democratic Leadership Council, 1994).

47. Eliminating those who did not express a preference or who preferred an independent or third-party candidate.

48. The figure would be 53 percent if preferences for candidates not on the ballot were ignored.

49. Martin Wattenberg, "The 1994 Election: Perot Voters and the Republican Shift," paper presented at the annual meeting of the American Political Science Association, August 31–September 3, 1995.

50. See also David W. Brady, John F. Cogan, and Douglas Rivers, *How the Republicans Captured the House* (Palo Alto, Calif.: Hoover Institution, 1995), for evidence that level of turnout was not a significant predictor of Republican gains.

Chapter Four

1. Robin Toner, "Middle America; Coming Home from the Revolution," *New York Times,* November 10, 1996, sec. 4, p. 1.

2. Various NBC News/*Wall Street Journal* and CNN/*USA Today*/Gallup polls, November 1994–February 1995.

3. NBC News/*Wall Street Journal* poll, May 1996; CNN/*USA Today*/Gallup polls, May 9–12, 1996.

4. NBC/*Wall Street Journal* poll, September 16–19, 1995.

5. See Thomas B. Edsall, "Confrontation Is the Key to Clinton's Popularity," *Washington Post,* December 24, 1995, for data and a lucid discussion of the evolution of the Democrats' battle with the Republicans.

6. See, for example, the data in the CNN/*USA Today*/Gallup poll of November 6–8, 1995, as well as the NBC/*Wall Street Journal* trial heat series referenced in Ruy Teixeira and Joel Rogers, "Volatile Voters: Declining Living Standards and Non-College-Educated Whites," Working Paper 116 (Washington, D.C.: Economic Policy Institute, August 8, 1996). See also *Who Joined the Democrats? Understanding the 1996 Election Results,* Briefing Paper (Washington, D.C.: Economic Policy Institute).

7. Of course, two other Democratic presidents—Truman and Johnson—have been elected as incumbents since Roosevelt. However, they succeeded to the presidency due to death of the sitting president and did not initially win election in their own right.

8. For a more elaborate analysis making essentially the same point, see Michael R. Alvarez and Jonathan Nagler, "Economics, Entitlements and Social Issues: Voter Choice in the 1996 Election," unpublished manuscript, Department of Political Science, University of California, Riverside, 1997.

9. "New kind of Democrat": CNN/*USA Today*/Gallup polls, July 7–9, 1995, and May 9–12, 1996; Clinton's approach to issues: NBC/*Wall Street Journal* polls, October 1994 and October 1996; "tax and spend Democrat": *Los Angeles Times* poll, October 24–27, 1996.

10. Joseph P. Kahn, "The True-Life Adventures of Soccer Mom," *Boston Globe*, October 30, 1996, F1.

11. 1996 VNS exit poll data.

12. The 1996 Census Voter Supplement data indicated that about 71 percent of voters in the 1996 election were non-college-educated. For a detailed discussion, see the beginning of Chapter 5.

13. Based both on a shift-share analysis of changes in Clinton support rates and on a breakdown of new Clinton voters by education as determined by the exit poll (data were reweighted to reflect the education distribution of voters as measured by the 1996 Census Voter Supplement data). The estimate is also supported by results from the Greenberg/CAF survey indicating that 78 percent of new Clinton voters were working class.

14. Too few Hispanics participated in this survey to permit valid estimates of their levels of concern.

15. See Barry Bluestone and Stephen Rose, *The Unmeasured Labor Force: The Growth in Work Hours*, Public Policy Brief 39 (Annandale-on-Hudson, N.Y.: Jerome Levy Economics Institute, 1998), for a detailed analysis of this phenomenon.

16. National Election Studies data.

17. Quoted in David Broder, "Triangulated at Last," *Washington Post*, December 15, 1996, p. C7.

18. Thomas Edsall, "Clinton Built New Base; House Democrats Didn't," *Washington Post*, November 10, 1996, p. A22.

19. See Chapter 5 for an extensive discussion of this point.

20. Non-Hispanic white. In some Census data, Hispanics are included in data for whites, but in the CD data it is possible to make whites and Hispanics separate categories, as they are in common usage and in most surveys, including the exit polls.

21. Class (education) data based on voting-age population (VAP) only. Note that race data for CDs cannot be disaggregated by age but should generally deflate the white figures from their VAP levels, since the black and, especially, Hispanic populations tend to be younger than the white population.

22. While expressed in 1998 dollars, this income figure and the others cited here have nevertheless been taken from the 1990 Census, which, in turn, captured household income in 1989. This is less of a problem than it might appear, however, since the most recently released Census Bureau data on income, from the March 1999 CPS, shows that real median income in 1998 was only 2 percent more than in 1989. Therefore, on average, the 1990 figures provide a reasonable rough estimate of the income situation in these CDs in the late 1990s.

23. Since 1990, the non-Hispanic white proportion of the population has fallen about 3 percentage points, from 75.6 percent to 72.5 percent. Similarly, since 1990, the proportion of the population (twenty-five years and older) with four years or more of college has increased about 3 points, from 21.3 percent to 24.4 percent. These changes suggest that, on average, the 1990 Census data on CDs overstates the former and understates the latter, but not by enough to change the basic pattern and story discussed here.

24. Or, more properly, the *average* median in these CDs. The technically correct specification is simplified here for clarity of exposition.

Chapter Five

1. David Broder, "Three Puzzles," *Washington Post,* January 5, 2000, p. A21.

2. When we use the terms *union* or *unionized* to refer to voters in this chapter, unless otherwise specified we are really referring to being in a *union household*—that is, a household where at least one union member is present. Counting union households is the standard way of assessing union influence on the vote, and in cases involving certain important surveys—the exit polls, for example—it is the only information collected on unions and the individual voter.

3. In the discussion that follows, we use the percentage of voters in each category based on 1996 data. This is both for clarity of expositon and because the election closely folllowing the book's publication will be the 2000 Presidential election. The distribution of voters from the last

presidential election, rather than the last off-year election, is probably a better guide for thinking about this election, so we present the 1996 data here.

4. In addition, statistical models indicate that strong union support for Democrats, controlling for the characteristics of union voters, is a long-standing feature of the American electorate and has not attenuated noticeably in recent years (contrary to assertions in the press, particularly by conservative commentators). That is, even though union support for Democrats has gone through some ups and downs (for example, in 1994), union Democratic support has continued to be about the same amount higher than that of the general public, once the race, income, educational level, and other characteristics of union voters are taken into account. Thus, the union "premium" for the Democrats is alive and well.

5. This figure is slightly lower than the one in published reports based on exit poll data, due to our reweighting of the exit poll data to reflect the distribution of union voters indicated by the Census data. In addition, our other categories reflect a reweighting of the exit poll data to align the distribution of voters by education with that indicated by the Census data. (For more details, see the Appendix.)

6. These figures are all inflated due to the problem of overreporting in the Census survey. (Again, see the Appendix.)

7. Note that even increasing union turnout rates in individual elections is not that easy. The AFL-CIO tried very hard to do so in 1998 and pointed to exit poll data that showed the proportion of union household voters increasing from 14 percent in 1994 to 23 percent in 1998. However, as the VNS exit pollsters themselves have acknowledged, this change is probably attributable to changed question wording in 1998, which made it more likely that union household voters would report their union affiliation. This interpretation is supported by Bureau of the Census data that show turnout among union members actually declining from 1994 to 1998, pretty much in line with the population-wide decline in turnout between the two elections. Moreover, both Census data and National Election Studies (NES) data, where question wording has been stable, show the union percentage of voters fluctuating in a narrow range between 1988 and the present (17 to 21 percent in the Census data, 18 to 21 percent in the NES data).

8. See Michael Goldfield, *The Decline of Organized Labor in the United States* (Chicago: University of Chicago Press, 1987), and Lawrence Mishel,

Jared Bernstein, and John Schmitt, *The State of Working America, 1998–99* (Ithaca, N.Y.: Cornell University Press, 1999). Adduced elsewhere are data that make the decline seem larger, but this apparent outcome may reflect figures based on union density in the *nonagricultural workforce*, which was quite a bit higher than that in the overall workforce in the 1950s and early 1960s (see Goldfield, table 1). In any event there is no consistent time series before 1973, so one is forced to rely on somewhat mismatched data series to estimate the decline in union density.

9. This figure is based on the authors' analysis of 1960–96 NES data.

10. This is the level of expected support that political scientists ascribed to the Democrats in the days when the New Deal coalition dominated American politics. It meant that Democrats had 53 percent of the vote for openers in most elections, which the Republicans then had to whittle down. Obviously, in many elections they succeeded—but it was an uphill struggle, and Democrats tended naturally to win more elections and dominate national politics.

11. See Michael Frisby, "Both Parties Take Stock of Jump in Black Male Turnout," *Wall Street Journal,* February 13, 1997, p. A20, for discussion.

12. See the Appendix for a description of these Census Voter Supplement data. Note also that we are talking here about all blacks, not just nonunion blacks. The reason is that the Census data do not permit a clean partition between union household and nonunion household blacks. However, there is no reason to think that these trends would look any different if the analysis was confined to nonunion blacks. In addition, the claims about increased black turnout—and Hispanic turnout, in the next section—concern these minority groups as a whole, so nothing is lost in terms of testing the conventional wisdom.

13. These figures are based on the authors' analysis of 1998 Bureau of the Census Voter Supplement data.

14. It is also worth noting that sharp increases in black turnout, even if one could attain them and simultaneously prevent countermobilization of other groups, would have less of a political impact than many suppose. There are several reasons for this, chiefly having to do with the relatively small population weight of blacks and the mathematics of increasing turnout. For extensive discussion of these issues, see Ruy Teixeira, *The Disappearing American Voter* (Washington, D.C.: Brookings, 1992), chapter 3.

15. Even in California, where the most dramatic changes in the Hispanic vote were supposed to have occurred, the overall increase in the Hispanic vote was just 156,000.

16. U.S. Bureau of the Census, *Population Projections of the United States by Age, Sex, Race and Hispanic Origin* (U.S. Department of Commerce, P25-1130, 1996).

17. In the *very* long run—the year 2050—the projections suggest that Hispanics will comprise more than a fifth—22.4 percent—of the voting-age population (VAP). In the more politically relevant short run, however, the projections show the Hispanic share of the VAP in the presidential election year of 2008 as just 11.7 percent. These are very important changes; but it is ridiculous, both analytically and politically, to lose sight of how long a time frame they unfold on.

18. The assumption here is that, as the Hispanic share of the VAP increases, the Hispanic share of voters will increase at the same rate it did between 1992 and 1996 (a 1 percent increase in voter share accompanied by a 1.6 percent increase in VAP share). Since this rate was fast by historical standards, the estimate given here is perhaps a generous one. But in any event, even if one assumed a *faster* rate of increase in the Hispanic vote share in the future—for example, a 1 percent increase in Hispanic vote share for every 1 percent increase in the Hispanic VAP—it would not make much difference to the estimated effect on the Democratic vote: It would go from an increase of slightly under 1 percent to an increase of slightly over 1 percent.

19. See Paul Starr, "An Emerging Democratic Majority," in Stanley B. Greenberg and Theda Skocpol, eds., *The New Majority: Toward a Popular Progressive Politics* (New Haven, Conn.: Yale University Press, 1997), for more discussion, as well as for a generally more optimistic view of the potential political impact of Hispanic population growth.

20. William A. Galston and Elaine C. Kamarck, "Five Realities That Will Shape Twentieth Century Politics," *Blueprint: Ideas for a New Century* (Washington, D.C.: Democratic Leadership Council, Fall 1998).

Chapter Six

1. "Economic Growth: Hey, What About Us?" *Business Week*, December 27, 1999.

2. See Pew Research Center, "Optimism Reigns, Technology Plays Key Role," Washington, D.C., October 24, 1999; Mark Penn, "Choosing the

New Economy," *Blueprint: Ideas for a New Century* (Washington, D.C.: Democratic Leadership Council, Winter 1998); and Program on International Policy Attitudes, *Americans on Globalization: A Summary of U.S. Findings*, on-line report, School of Public Affairs, University of Maryland (www.pipa.org).

3. See Pew Research Center, *Retropolitics, The Political Typology: Version 3.0* (Washington, D.C.: Pew Research Center, 1999), and Andrew Kohut, "Globalization and the Wage Gap," *New York Times*, December 3, 1999, p. A31.

4. See Ruy Teixeira, "Happy with Health Care," *The American Prospect*, December 20, 1999, for supporting data.

5. Pew Research Center, *Retropolitics—The Political Typology: Version 3.0*, Washington, D.C., November 1999.

6. See, for example, the polling data in Mark Penn, "Choosing the New Economy," *Blueprint: Ideas for a New Century* (Washington, D.C.: Democratic Leadership Council, Winter 1998), and Mark Penn, "A Hunger for Reform," *Blueprint: Ideas for a New Century* (Washington, D.C.: Democratic Leadership Council, Fall 1999).

7. Near the top of the 1980s business cycle (1988), International Survey Research found that 73 percent of workers believed they could count on job security if they did a good job. But in the 1990s business cycle, the number had reached only 56 percent by mid-1998, the eighth year of the expansion and a period of very fast growth and tight labor markets.

8. Lawrence Mishel, Jared Bernstein, and John Schmitt, *The State of Working America, 1998–99* (Ithaca, N.Y.: Cornell University Press, 1999), pp. 235–240.

9. For good data on all these points, see Program on International Policy Attitudes, *Americans on Globalization: A Summary of U.S. Findings*, on-line report, School of Public Affairs, University of Maryland (www.pipa.org).

10. See Lake Sosin Snell Perry and Associates' February 1998 poll for The National Partnership for Women and Families and the *Los Angeles Times* May 1999 poll on Child Care in California.

11. Dean Baker, "What's New in the 1990's?" in Jeff Madrick, ed., *Perspectives on Economics* (New York: The Century Foundation, forthcoming). *Consumer debt* is defined as the ratio of nonmortgage consumer debt to disposable income.

12. This situation reflects the typical tendency of U.S. policy makers to mistake a secondary cause for a period of prosperity—in this case,

deficit reduction—for a primary one and ascribe near-mystical powers to that secondary cause. See John Judis, *The Paradox of American Democracy: Elites, Special Interests and the Betrayal of Public Trust* (New York: Pantheon, 2000).

13. See Barry Bluestone and Bennett Harrison, *Growing Prosperity: The Battle for Growth and Equity in the 21st Century* (New York: Houghton-Mifflin/The Century Foundation, 2000), for an extended argument that the role of deficit reduction in producing late-1990s prosperity is vastly exaggerated.

14. See, for example, Henry Aaron, "The Great Pretender," *Washington Post*, November 8, 1999, p. A21. And for a detailed treatment of the issue of long-term Social Security solvency, see Dean Baker and Mark Weisbrot, *Social Security: The Phony Crisis* (Chicago: University of Chicago Press, 1999).

15. See Rudolph G. Penner, Sandeep Solanki, Eric Toder, and Michael Wesner, "Saving the Surplus to Save Social Security: What Does It Mean?" Retirement Project Brief No. 7 (Washington, D.C.: Urban Institute, October, 1999).

16. "Clinton's Loss of Domestic Initiative," *Washington Times*, November 29, 1999, p. A17.

17. See Edith Rasell, "Paying for a Universal, Publicly-Financed Health Insurance System for Children" (Washington, D.C.: Economic Policy Institute, unpublished, 1999), for a detailed estimate. See also Benjamin Aldrich-Moodie, "Universal Health Coverage for Children," Idea Brief series (New York: Century Foundation, 2000).

18. Jacob Hacker, "Bradley Does Healthcare," *The Nation*, October 25, 1999.

19. See Barry Bluestone and Bennett Harrison, *Growing Prosperity: The Battle for Growth and Equity in the 21st Century* (New York: Houghton-Mifflin/The Century Foundation, 2000), chapter 8, for a brief description of how such a program might work.

20. See Richard Kahlenberg, *The Remedy: Class, Race and Affirmative Action* (New York: Basic Books, 1996), for a detailed treatment of this idea.

21. See Richard Kahlenberg, *All Together Now: The Case for Class Integration of the Public Schools*, forthcoming.

22. See Edith Rasell, *Paying for a Universal, Publically-Financed Health Insurance System for Children*, Washington, D.C.: Economic Policy Institute, unpublished manuscript, 1999; and Benjamin Aldrich-Moodie, *Universal Health Coverage for Children*, New York: Century Foundation, Idea

Brief No. 4, 2000. Bradley's plan had other serious problems as well, such as eliminating Medicaid without adequate replacement funding. See Ronald Brownstein, "Auditing the Sprawling Spreadsheet of Bradley's Health Care Proposal," *Los Angeles Times*, December 27, 1999.

23 See Eric Rhodes, *A Universal Preschool*, New York: Century Foundation, Idea Brief series, 2000.

Afterword

1. See Ruy Teixeira, "Gore's Tenuous Bond with Working Voters", *American Prospect*, 11:24, November 20, 2000.

2. See Jeffrey Bell's and Frank Cannon's instructive article in the *Weekly Standard*, November 27, 2000.

Appendix

1. Samuel Popkin and Michael McDonald, "Who Votes?" *Blueprint: Ideas for a New Century* (Washington, D.C.: Democratic Leadership Council, Fall 1998).

2. See Brian Silver, Barbara Anderson, and Paul Abramson, "Who Over-reports Voting?," *American Political Science Review* 80 (1986): 613–624. A check of 1988 validated vote data from the NES showed basically the same pattern. However, as vote data were not validated for the 1992 NES, a similar check could not be performed for that year.

Acknowledgments

We would like to thank Tim Bartlett of Basic Books for doing an excellent job of editing our manuscript and his Perseus Books colleague, Leo Wiegman, for taking an early and much-appreciated interest in our book project. Roger Hickey, John Judis, Richard Kahlenberg, Michael Lind and Lawrence Mishel read the manuscript and provided helpful comments. Others too numerous to mention, including the entire Washington, D.C. "new synthesis" group, provided useful reactions to earlier versions of the argument in this book.

Teixeira's research for the book was conducted at the Economic Policy Institute, whose support he gratefully acknowledges. Without that support, this book never would have happened.

Financial support for this project was also crucial. We thank the Russell Sage Foundation, the Arca Foundation and the Carnegie Corporation of New York for their generous support.

Clerical and research assistance for the book was provided by Catherine Bloniarz, Danielle Gao, Monica Hernandez, Stephanie Scott-Steptoe, Solon Simmons and David Webster, who all did a fine job. National Election Studies data were provided by the Inter-university Consortium for Political and Social Research, exit poll data by the Voter News Service and Current Population Survey data by the U.S. Bureau of the Census. Jared Bernstein, Keating Holland, John Mollenkopf and Stephen Rose were kind enough to provide other data used at various points in our analysis. We also benefitted from unpublished manuscripts supplied to us by Clem Brooks, Martin Gilens and Tom Smith.

INDEX